Other books by Diana R. Zimmerman

When the Roll is Called a Pyonder:
Tales of a Mennonite Childhood

Marry a Mennonite Boy and Make Pie

Early Reader Response to *A Lucky Breath*

"Diana Zimmerman's lyrical memoir, a tale of walking away and returning, kept me returning each time I attempted to walk away. The short chapters interpose her memories of a foreign culture that privileged Americans can't imagine with the story of a broken marriage. Zimmerman's spare prose hides its melancholy behind concrete images like those of chickens roosting in trees and clothes washed by hand in a cement wash sink. A compulsive read about love affairs, despair, lost paths, raw beauty, and the will to try again when you get up in the morning."

—Jeremy Garber, Methodist Theological Seminary of Ohio

"Opening with a mental map of her Costa Rican community, Zimmerman lays out her journey through a rugged landscape toward a place of home and forgiveness. She navigates her loves and her losses with a brutal, yet beautiful introspection. She does this with a lyricism that "retains the melody that once was losing its tune." This is no ordinary memoir of leaving an abusive relationship. It is an adventure in beguiling honesty and bursts of beauty."

—Hope Nisly, Emeritus Librarian, Fresno Pacific University

"Diana Zimmerman writes with heart and passion. Her personal reflections on leaving an abusive marriage, her understanding of family life and culture in Costa Rica, and her personal stories make this a rich and captivating read. Zimmerman's words point to the complicated nature of justice for the vulnerable amid questions of love and loss."

—Amy Gingerich, Herald Press

Critical Praise for *Marry a Mennonite Boy and Make Pie*

"*Marry a Mennonite Boy and Make Pie* is a funny, moving, insightful memoir about early adulthood and the struggle to reconcile Mennonite identity with one's encounters with the World. It depicts the kind of narrative shared by so many Mennonites in the late twentieth and early twenty-first centuries, told honestly and unashamedly."
—Daniel Shank Cruz, Utica College

"There comes a time when each of us need to decide just how close or how distant we need to be from the world of our childhood to become what feels true for our adult selves. This book perfectly captures that time."
—Sherri Klassen, University of Toronto

"Diana Zimmerman exposes the emotions that accompany the coming-of-age struggles of a Mennonite woman who eagerly seeks to learn about the diverse and multicultural world that becomes her new reality. That struggle eventually finds a peaceful haven in connections with others who are on the same journey as they face, together, a future filled with new discoveries."
—Lauren Friesen, PhD, University of Michigan

"Diana writes an entertaining, honest, coming to age memoir of a young woman who struggles to honor her TRUTH in the midst of the ever-present Mennonite culture. While some people never chose to leave the 'safe and certain' Mennonite Culture, Diana earnestly claws her way through to her own truth."
—Victoria L. Creighton, Clinical Director, Pine River Institute

"Diana Zimmerman's literary snapshots bring a lost world to life. Standing on the brink of the Internet era, her youthful characters struggle with faith, friendship, and the future in ways that are hard to imagine now, except through a book like this. A consummate act of memory."
—Sofia Samatar, author of *A Stranger in Olondria*

Copyright © 2023 Diana R. Zimmerman. All rights reserved.
dianarenee.com

Published by Workplay Publishing, 2023.
Newton, KS 67114

workplaypublishing.com

ISBN 1-7343946-5-X
Cover design and interior layout by André Swartley
Cover photo by Fabian Reitmeier
Author photos by Hernan Heredia

PRINTED IN THE UNITED STATES OF AMERICA

A Lucky Breath

a memoir

Diana R. Zimmerman

WORKPLAY PUBLISHING

Table of Contents

Prologue I: The Map	12
Prologue II: 1991	14
Part I: The End	16
Part II: Fugitive	40
Part III: Nicaragua	87
Part IV: Atlanta	140
Part V: Puntarenas	186
Part VI: San Francisco de Dos Ríos	205
Part VII: Tibás	223
Part VIII: A Solid Door	253
Part IV: The Beginning	285
Afterword I	289
Afterword II	290

Dedicated to Rebeca

my sister

who lent me a blanket when I was cold

Author's Note

This is a work of memory. Where memory fails, fiction is employed. And, as memory is subjective, it may or may not be historically acurate. Many names of people and places are changed.

Prologue I: The Map

Draw this:

    Start with a blank page.
    Draw an X in the middle.
    This is Los Ríos, hidden in the hills where the rest of the world cannot find it.
    Beside it, to the west, mark Santa Cecilia.
    Santa Cecilia is a small town like Los Ríos, a few kilometers further from nowhere.
    Circle the space east of Los Ríos.
    This is nowhere.
    Coyotes live there, mythical creatures, birds, rice fields, and giant trees.
    Draw a road from Los Ríos to Santa Cecilia.
    Draw the road continuing from Santa Cecilia to Santa Cruz, which you will mark on the far western edge of the world.

It is a dusty cowboy town with a few paved streets, grocery stores, a clinic, the electric company, scrappy bars, farm supply stores, and the local stockyards.
Buses originate here, and return.
Nicoya, to the south, and Liberia, to the north, are the two poles at the far ends of our planet.
Connect them with roads from Santa Cruz.

Everything else is far away and has a map of its own.

Prologue II: 1991

When I first stepped foot in Costa Rica, I was twenty years old.
The college I attended requires students to study a language and it sends them, for a semester, to a country that speaks it. I chose Spanish because it seemed the most practical, and because I could spend a winter somewhere warm.

In February 1991, I boarded a bus from Costa Rica's capital to Los Ríos to learn pottery techniques from indigenous potters. This was my assignment. The mother and the grandmother who hosted me demonstrated the process again and again until my fingers understood. I learned to work the clay into vases.

I fell in love with Los Ríos long before I met Enrique. I loved how the moon hangs low over the plaza on windy nights, hot black coffee brewed over a guacimo fire, and the indecent colors of hibiscus flowers. The earthenware molded by hands that hold the knowledge of its shaping in their veins captivated me. Enrique was far away working in the Caribbean banana plantations then.

The people took me to the places where they pry the clay from the earth, sacred places to the ancestors who passed these traditions through generations. I felt the presence of old secrets, both strange and familiar, and an inexplicable sense of belonging. A boy, a potter who etched delicate images of winged serpents, said he loved me and asked me not to leave.

I did leave, but Los Ríos drew me back.

Part 1: The End

Up until that morning, I can't know whether or not I will lose my nerve and stay with him.
People do that.
I think I will not, but I can't know.
I awaken before dawn and lie immobile, listening to the roosters crow throughout Los Ríos.
You don't sleep well the night before you leave your husband.
You awaken in the dark and you and wait for dawn.
You hear everything.

Enrique is sleeping beside me, far away in some safe place where he doesn't imagine what will happen today.
I want to slide my arm around his ribs and nestle into the familiar warmth of his broad back this last time.
But I don't.
I promised.
I promised myself I would never do that again.
He doesn't accept uninvited affection.
He confuses it with sex, a prerogative he regards as his own.

It is better to suffer this sad ache in my chest than his angry elbows and heels in my belly pushing me back.
Machismo, as it turns out, is alive and well in the villages of Central America.
My first-world origin has not made me immune to it.
I listen to the roosters and the wind, to the dogs barking at night creatures, to the slow breathing of my husband.

Last night we danced like in the old days.
We danced any place we heard music back in the times when it was impossible to be near each other in any other way.
Back when we believed a thing you don't say remains a secret.
We pretended it was accident bringing us together in those crowded salones de baile and dusty bars.
We hoped everyone would believe us.
I tried to stop myself from seeing him.
I honestly tried.
But the vertigo created by the pull between us, when I attempted to resist it, threatened to knock me off my feet and catapult me into the sky.

While we dance on our last night together, a wild giddiness creeps over me.
I can see the future.
I know something no one else does.
Tonight I am still Enrique's wife, and we dance.
He holds me against him and spins me around and around.
I follow.
One last time, I follow him.
He pushes me, pulls me, and I stay with his rhythm.
Flawlessly.
I know him.
And I know that now there is no turning back, that in the morning I am going to get up and walk away.

A LUCKY BREATH

Flip the breaker.
Blackout.
The end.

Dance with me, baby.
Now or never.
I'm leaving you in the morning.
See if you feel like dancing then.

I am furious.
I am strong as cast iron.
I am already far away.
The decision happened months ago and I have proceeded with calm.

I've needed time to become certain it is the right thing to do and that I am capable of it.
I am certain.
I am capable.

My family will approve of me leaving my husband when I confess his unfaithfulness and my unsafety.
During these three years I tell them nothing of it.
Shame sickens me.
I hear their silent thoughts.
They are thinking that they knew all along I would be sorry for marrying him.
I don't want to prove their unvoiced warnings to be right.
I do it anyway.
I don't want to explain, but I have to.
They will think to themselves that of course this would never work.
No one ever says this to me, but I know they think it.
My pride is a hard swallow.

I swallow it and write a letter to my mother and father.
In the place that I come from, good women don't leave their husbands.
I explain to them that Enrique is unkind to me and unfaithful.
They tell me to be safe and to come home.

And there is Enrique's family, who is my family too, now.
I love them.
I beg their forgiveness for what I am about to do.
There is nothing to forgive, they say.
He is impossible.
We love you.
Please go.
You are free.

I form a plan.
A friend gives me directions to her farm hidden in the mountains.
When I am ready, I will put my things in the truck and drive away.
Safe at the farm, I will purchase a plane ticket back to the United States.
My sister who lives in Atlanta prepares the extra bedroom for me.
I wait for an indication that it is time to go, and the indication comes.
I call my friend to tell her I am ready.
She checks her calendar and says the house will be open on Monday, the 27th day of March.

I have done everything.
This is that day.

Angel was the only person in the family that I told about my plan to leave Enrique. I told him ahead of time, while I waited for the right moment to go. He encouraged me.

True to his name, Angel came often to check on me as if he were my younger brother instead of Enrique's. He wandered across the yard between our houses at dusk to chat with me as I watered our plants, making sure I was alright. We talked about family happenings, town gossip, and about Enrique. His anger. His absences. His women that no one would tell me about but I knew they were there. Enrique had become unbearable in the months since we came back from our six-month working visit to the USA. He shouted more than ever, then thundered away in the truck leaving dust clouds in the road.

Angel wondered what all the tantrums were about. I said I didn't know. What were they ever about? Nothing. Everything. Enrique was always angry with me when he was home, but mostly he wasn't home. He wouldn't say where he went, and stormed away in a rage if I asked. Before, when I cared, I was hurt by these things. I spent enormous amounts of energy trying not to provoke his anger. That was back when I still thought we could be happy together if I tried harder. I didn't care anymore if he was angry or about how much noise he made.

Angel looked at me shaking his head. "Qué hace usted aquí?" he asked, searing me with his gaze. "Él no va a cambiar," he said. "Váyase. Váyase y sea feliz."

Enrique was wonderful in the beginning. He was my best friend and valiant lover, so when the ship I thought was unsinkable began to fall apart, I found sections to cling to as long as I could. Now there was nothing left except a small white house with a blue tile floor, a gray pick-up truck, and torrents of insults. We couldn't rebuild our broken bond because Enrique liked things the way they were now. He would go on like this forever. He was happy with a marriage where he shouted at his wife, disappeared with friends and girlfriends, then returned home when his wife was supposed to be blissfully sleeping in a house full of appliances: a TV, a washer, a refrigerator...

So, I told Angel my secret. "Lo voy a hacer," I said. I explained I didn't know when, but that there was a house I could go to in the mountains where I would be safe. My plan was ready; I knew everything except the moment. I was waiting for it.

He hugged me, both happy and sad, and said, "Bien."

On the night before I left, I whispered to Angel that I was ready to go in the morning. I asked him for one favor: help me move my writing desk out of the house before I go. The desk is the only thing I owned that I could neither take with me, toss into a burn pile in the back yard, nor bear to abandon. Enrique and Angel's brother, Lenny the carpenter, made it for me, and I wanted Angel to have it. I couldn't think of leaving my beloved writing desk for Enrique to destroy in anger or by neglect. I couldn't have imagined, then, that Angel would keep it for me and one day give it back to me to put in my new apartment.

I believed I would leave Costa Rica and never come back.

A LUCKY BREATH

Enrique awakens.
He stands, finds pants, and walks out of the house to feed the dog and water the plants.
It is the dry season.
This is how all days begin.
I lie still.
My heart pounds.
I fear it is written on my forehead that, after all the lies Enrique has told me, today I am the deceiver with the false face of calm.
Will he look at me and know?
I tell myself he will not.
Nothing must be unusual about this March Monday morning.

As I have done every day for these three years, I get up and make coffee.
I shower and dress, put sweetbread and butter on the table and pour the coffee.
I stir milk and two scoops of sugar into Enrique's cup.
I call to him that breakfast is ready.
We sit at the table and eat together.
His dark curls are wet from the shower and smell of the hair gel he loves.
I watch his deft brown fingers as the grip the coffee cup.
I watch his jaw move as he chews.
Enrique is beautiful.
I want to act normal, but I can't breathe.
I ask Enrique what he is going to do today.
He hates that question.
He snorts that he is going to work, annoyed that I have asked him to state the obvious.

He gulps the last swallow of coffee and pushes back from the table.
I say I have to go to town this morning.
I say this because I will drive our truck down the road past the pottery cooperative where he works when I leave.
I don't want this to surprise him.
Surprises spark his explosive possessiveness, and I would rather be ignored.
He gives me money and tells me to bring him batteries for the flashlight and food for the dog.
I lay the money on the table.
I kiss him goodbye before he walks out the door—a little peck of a kiss on the lips.
He hates these formalities, but might notice if I don't insist.
I always insist.
I would love for him to crush me against his chest in an embrace like he used to.
He doesn't.
Enrique gets on his bicycle and rides away.
His red shirt disappears around the corner into the trees.
My coffee has gone cold.

There are no last-minute decisions today.
Every movement I will make now is premeditated.
Enrique isn't aware that objects in the house have been shuffled.
My clothes are separated into what I will take and what I will leave.
I've gone through my books, notebooks, and papers.
A fire in the back yard last week released the things I can neither stand to leave nor afford to take with me.
Better to send them back into the universe myself than to imagine Enrique destroying them in rage.
Trash fires are unsuspicious.

My luggage is ready in minutes.
I know what goes in each box, each suitcase.
In my mind, I have rehearsed these moments a thousand times.
Time will be important.
Enrique must not catch me leaving him.
Enrique loves nothing on earth as much as our pick-up truck.
But my name is on the title and it is coming with me.
Enrique will have the house and everything in it so I feel I am not unfair.
I don't know what Enrique will do if he catches me trying to leave him with the truck.
Maybe scream horrible insults.
Maybe cry and beg me to stay.
Maybe hurt me.
He could simply stand behind the truck so that I can't move it.
He could break the windows, slash the tires.
There are a hundred ways to foil my plan.
I have imagined them all.

I am mostly afraid that he will break my resolve.
I am afraid if he begs me to stay, I will give in.
I have before.
I love him.

So I run away like a criminal, hiding from what Enrique might do to me and what I might do to myself.
I am trembling and sweating cold as I push my belongings into suitcases and boxes.
This efficiency makes leaving my life look easy.
It isn't.

After three months of waiting, I got my signal that announced it was time to go.

I went looking for trouble one day and I found it in a little square package in the back of Enrique's wallet. The package was dog-eared, as if it had been there for a long time. I was angry. I was amused. I was taking birth control pills; I knew it wasn't for me. I was curious. How stupid can he be? What's the first thing any suspicious wife would look for? And where is the first place she would look for it? I thought about taking the condom out and throwing it away. I thought about cutting it in half and putting it back. I thought about buying a syringe and injecting it with hot sauce. I thought about pitching a fit.

I decided to wait.

All things considered, a condom in the wallet was enough to warrant me walking out and never coming back. More than enough. Enrique had promised me on the life of his mother and children that he would change, as we sat on the grass under the tree outside the airport last year. If I came home, he was going to stop being mean, absent, and seeing other women. Forever. But he was only kind for the short time until we left for our trip to the USA, and he'd begun disappearing again the minute we got back. He'd thrown me at David during the Fiestas in Santa Cruz so he could go off mysteriously every night. Only a few weeks ago he went to see Sandrita and didn't come home. I wished I could cheat on him too, but I couldn't. I would have lost the respect of everyone in the family and in the town. I would have lost my self-respect. On one hand, men aren't supposed to cheat, but on the other, they are allowed to. They are secretly respected more if they do. Machismo is like that.

There is only one reason a man carries condoms in the back

of his wallet. Possessed by morbid curiosity, I kept quiet. And I started packing the suitcase that I stored under the bed beside my desk in the extra bedroom. Occasionally, the condom disappeared and was replaced by another—sometimes immediately replaced, or sometimes a few days later. Once, there was no condom in the wallet for so many days that I feared I had waited too long. I couldn't very well storm out of our marriage in a scene of righteous indignation over condoms if there weren't any. Eventually, another one appeared.

    I sorted through my clothes and the things in my desk drawers, the kitchen drawers, boxes I kept in the extra bedroom. What I wanted to take with me went into the luggage under the bed. I re-arranged things so it wouldn't seem like anything was missing. There was no hurry. I would recognize the moment when it came, and I would be ready when it did.

    "Póngame esto en la billetera," Enrique said, and pushed a business card at me without looking away from the TV. A hardware store in Santa Cruz.

    The wallet lay across the room on a small table. And I recognized, with a calm and terrible clarity, that this was my moment. Just like that. Delivered to me as easily and as naturally as anything ever could be. This was my cue to begin the scene I rehearsed.

    God help me.

    My heart pounded and I felt dizzy. With my back to Enrique, I picked up his wallet, breathed deep, and opened it. I paused with the wallet in my hands. By now the imprint of a ring was pressed into the leather, clearly visible without even opening the fold. Rage boiled inside me, the rage I had smothered for weeks and months and years. I didn't need to act the part—I was livid. I slipped my fingers into the wallet, pulled out an infuriatingly new-looking condom, wheeled with sincere ire and demanded, "¿Qué es eso?!"

    Enrique responded in instant fury.

"*Qué cree que es!? ¡¿Por qué anda revisando mi billetera?!*"
"*Para qué lo ocupa?*" I countered. "*No es para mí!*"
"*Usted es una idiota! No le importa! Es mi billetera!*"
"*Sí que me importa! Usted es mi esposo! Y usted me dijo de poner algo en su billetera.*"

He couldn't argue with that, so he changed his approach. But I knew his lies before he told them.

"*Pues, enójese si quiere,*" Enrique snorted. "*No me importa. No es para mí. Yo no los uso. Los vendo a los muchachos. Usted siempre piensa mal de mí!*" he threw in, trying to make the problem mine. He turned away from me, poorly feigning hurt feelings, and pretended to sulk.

"*Ah!*" I said, "*Le gustaría si encontrara usted condones en mi billetera y que yo le dijera que los estoy vendiendo?*" We weren't done. This time I wanted a fight and we were going to have it.

"*Qué me interesa?*" he answered. "*Hágalo!*"

"*Va a ver,*" I said, and the menace in my voice surprised me. "*Va a ver.*"

"*A ver qué?*" he shot back, daring me.

"*Yo no sé,*" I lied.

"*Va a ver usted!*" he warned darkly, thinking I was threatening to cheat on him.

I had every intention of cheating on him. Later. When I was too far away for him to ever catch me.

My husband the condom seller. I asked myself if it could be true, but I couldn't believe it for a minute. It wasn't the worst thing he'd done, but it was enough to prove to anyone who needed evidence that this marriage was a farce. The only one who needed one last piece of evidence was me.

The next day I called my friend to tell her I was ready to go to her mountain house. She said it would be available on Monday.

A LUCKY BREATH

It's seven in the morning.
The children are leaving for school.
They live with their mother in a little house on the other side of Enrique's parents' yard.
Through my window, I watch them as they run out the door and down the dusty road, backpacks bouncing on their shoulders.
I know I have to wait until the children are gone because I will never be able to say goodbye to them, never explain, never walk away.
I can walk away from my husband, but I can't walk away from his children.
Three little ones.
Carina is only in kindergarten.

I cross the dry yard that lies between our house and Enrique's parents' house.
The sun presses down on my shoulders like a hot iron.
María and Martín love me like their own blood.
They lament their son's behavior, so often save me from loneliness, and shelter me from his rages.
I hold a letter for them in my hand.

María is at the sink.
She turns to me when I enter, says, "Buenos días," and asks me how I slept.
I lie and say, "Muy bien."
And then, because I am too frightened and too torn for small talk, I simply say the day for the big trip has arrived.
María doesn't ask what big trip.
She melts into tears, clasps me to her, and weeps.

"Yo traté," she chokes out.
"Traté de decirle."
"Yo le dije, pero él no cambia."
My elderly father-in-law Martín, who is sitting at the table, begins to cry also, calling his son stupid and stubborn.
This second father to me is the most heartbroken of us all.
I tell them I am leaving now, quickly.
That I love Enrique, but can't live with him.
That I love them and nothing is their fault.
All the while I have one eye on the window, watching for a red shirt to come up the street.
If he comes back, I am caught now like a fly in a web.
Terror knots my stomach.
My hands tremble.
I give María the letter and walk away, misleadingly dry-eyed.
There is no crying for me today.
The crying came before and it comes after.
The center of this storm is dead calm.
I call Angel and he follows me back to my house.
We lift my desk and carry it to his room.

I cannot move fast enough.
But fear must not make me careless.
The pottery shop where Enrique works is on the way out of town on a hill above the street.
I can't drive by it with a load of luggage in the back of the pick-up truck.
I do not want Enrique to sense something odd.
I do not want to be chased.
Angel helps me push my bags and boxes into the cab.
I give him the phone number of the farm where I am going.
He can call from Los Ríos' only telephone later and I can tell him I'm alright.

A LUCKY BREATH

María and Martín will worry until they hear from me.
Angel hugs me and he is crying.
I am the only one who is somewhere far, far away—so far outside of myself that I watch it all from above my own shoulder.

When he came to pick María and me up at his grandmother's house on the banana plantation near Guapiles, Enrique the entrepreneur saw a chance to make some money. On the morning we left, he bought a mountain of green platanos. The trip from our home in the Pacific region to the Atlantic had taken María and me two days on buses, but in the truck we made it in one. Piled high with fruit, we couldn't stop for the night even if we wanted to without losing our precious cargo to sticky fingers.

Back home the next day, Enrique informed me at breakfast that it was my job to drive around Los Ríos and the surrounding towns selling the truckload of ripening fruit. I looked at him like he had finally lost his mind. He snorted, and growled that I had to do it, that he didn't have time, that he had to work in the pottery workshop. He told me the boys would help me, and his statements left no room for questions or refusals. It would be the way he said—the only variable over which I had control was how much he shouted at me before I gave in. So I didn't argue. I didn't care anymore. I was ready to leave him the minute I knew it was time. The honeymoon after our week apart was apparently over.

It was February 29. I remembered how, four years ago on the previous February 29, we went with Mateo to the mountain to gather the rock pigment called curiol that we needed for painting our pottery. Mateo was the first friend I'd made in Los Ríos, long before I knew Enrique, and now he was Enrique's best friend. I remembered how close Enrique and I felt to each other that day on the mountain even though speaking, up there, is considered bad luck. I didn't bring it up. We didn't speak much on this February 29 either, but not because it would chase away our luck. Our luck was long gone.

On that day, three weeks before I drove away forever in the same truck, Adán, Miguel and I bounced up and down the dusty roads in the scalding sun and searing wind, selling platanos. Adán and Miguel were 10 and 9. They sat in the truck bed scrapping as always, calling out, "Platanos, platanos!" as I directed us slowly past sleepy houses. Curious neighbors who got up from their pottery tables or from in front of their TV sets to see what was going on with the Campos boys and me, proffered a few colones for platanos straight from the Caribbean.

It felt surreal, like a dream. Driving around Los Ríos in my truck with my children like nothing was wrong. I wondered if I was seeing these people and places for the last time. Sometimes I wanted to cry. Sometimes I wanted to sing. I thought I might be going crazy.

Sooner or later—and probably sooner—Enrique was going to make a final mistake. He would get drunk again and hurt me or break things. He would go out at night and forget to come home. Someone would tell me a rumor about him sleeping with someone else. These were components of my life that I realized were not going to go away until I went away. So I waited for the next one—the one that would be my excuse to leave and not turn around.

By evening we only had enough platanos left for dinner.

I leave a note on the table with the money Enrique gave me.
The note quotes a song:
>   *Te quiero, pero no puedo soportarte.*
>   *Me voy a morir, pero será en otra parte.*
>   *No quiero que nuestros hijos ven tu ejemplo*
>   *y vuelven a hacer el daño que me haces tú.*

Then, I turn, walk out of my house, and close the door.
My little cat climbs into the cab of the truck.
He has never done this.
I take him out.
I must go alone.

I back out of my driveway onto the dusty road.
How many hundreds of times have I done this?
Now I will never do it again.
The last time and the first time, how alike they are, both new and unknown.
It feels like dying.
I am slipping out of my life into whatever lies beyond.

The sun is very hot in March and the trees are parched to their skeletons.
The dirt road and the sky are bleached white by the sun.
Now, I think, in a few minutes I will be safe.
Go.
My eyes are peeled for the first glimpse of a red shirt.
The pottery shop is a moment's bike ride from the house, and Enrique can return at any time for any reason.
All I want is to make it past the workshop.
What if I meet him riding toward me, and he motions for me

to stop?
What will I do?
Keep driving?
Stop?
Pretend not to see him?
I am weak with fear.
Everything is going exactly as planned.
It is 8:00 o'clock in the morning.
I am in the truck with my things.
Driving calmly.
It's going to be ok.
You can do this.
Just drive.
Just drive.

Around the corner, the plaza comes into view—the thing I love most about Los Ríos—that tidy communal space in the center of our universe.
I drive along the stripe of black pavement past the irrigated green plaza, the brown limbs of dormant trees, and the little white houses.
Pink and red flowers startle me with their frightening color.
Shapes, colors, and so much silence.
There is only the hum of the engine of the grey truck and the thumping of my terrified heart.
One more corner to go, the most dangerous one, which takes me in front of the workshop.
What if Enrique stands by the road and waves me to stop?
What if he notices the boxes and suitcases as I pass?
I fix my eyes on the road and promise myself that nothing in the world—nothing—can stop me now.
I am so close to my freedom he will have to chase me down and murder me to take it away.

This, I know, he will not do.

I round the corner, and Enrique isn't standing by the road.
Of course not.
Why would he?
He must be somewhere inside the workshop.
Working.
And so, in my relief and my anger, and with the bittersweet taste of revenge on my tongue, I tap the horn and wave, smiling.
And drive on past.
Bye.

I cross over the line from captive to fugitive.
And the next wave of fear begins.

A LUCKY BREATH

    I went with my mother-in-law María to the Caribbean region to visit her mother and siblings knowing I'd never be back that way again. I'd always wanted to go, but my Saturday teaching commitment at the University kept me from it. I wasn't teaching this semester, though. I used the excuse that Enrique and I had just gotten back from the United States and I wasn't ready. I said I needed a little time. I'd told the University maybe next semester, although I was sure I'd be gone by then.

    María and I took the bus to San José, spent the night with her son, Lenny, then took another bus to Guapiles in the morning. The cool mountain air of San José melted into a Caribbean steam bath. We waited a long time in Guapiles for the last decrepit bus to carry us through the rain out to the banana plantation. When we finally disembarked in the middle of nowhere, the clouds parted and we saw the sun beginning to set on our second day of travel. I was tired, sticky, and thirsty enough almost to wish that I had stayed home.

    María's mother Paula lived with her husband Chico and two of her many grandchildren, in an old-style wooden house lost in the endless green hills near the plantation. María's sisters and their families lived on the plantation in worker housing—horrifying little cement block boxes crammed together in ugly rows with muddy yards and laundry hanging from anywhere you could tie a piece of twine. In the neighborhoods on the banana plantation, there were too many children, not enough husbands, there was not enough money, and too much crime. But off the plantation by a lush ravine under the mango trees, Paula and Chico were alright. They had a cinnamon tree in the back yard by the sink where we washed our clothes, fresh yucca so soft I would never have imagined it, and pineapple plants everywhere. Anything left lying on the ground either decomposed instantly or sprung to life.

We stayed for ten days, and for ten days, it rained. Banana plants need immense amounts of water to produce fruit. This is their paradise. It rained in the morning while we were making our coffee. It rained while Yolanda, timid granddaughter, mopped the floors. It rained at lunch time and while we took afternoon naps. Rain fell while we fried our gallo pinto and platanos for dinner, and during the night came the torrents.

The wooden house was comprised of three bedrooms, a long rectangular living room, a porch in the front, and a kitchen tacked on the side. The kitchen had a dirt floor and a hand-built clay wood-burning hornilla for cooking. We lived on the porch. Paula and her husband Chico each had their own bedrooms. Paula said Chico snored, and Chico said Paula snored. There was plenty of room in the house, so they kept the peace that way. Besides, they had never been able to agree on a bed. Paula refused anything but a wooden bed frame with no mattress and no pillow. They hurt her back, she said. When she was young no one had mattresses, she said, and she didn't see why she needed one now. She preferred to cover with a sheet and sleep on the wooden slats. Chico wanted a mattress and pillow, but Paula would have none of it.

Yolanda and her little brother shared the third bedroom. Yolanda had come to live with her grandma when she was a barely more than a toddler. Her parents drank guaro when they weren't in the banana fields, and sometimes they forgot to save money for food for their little one. Paula simply took her one day and didn't give her back. The arrangement worked out for the best for everyone. Then the little boy was born. When his mama weaned him and went back to work, grandma Paula came for him, too.

The little boy lent his bed to María and went to sleep with Chico. Yolanda shared her little bed with me. We put our pillows at opposite ends and tried not to kick each other during the night. For as hot as it is during the sauna of daytime, nights are surprisingly cool under walls of falling water. The sound of it on the roof over the bed where Yolanda and I curled like kittens was as solid as if the air were made of cement. We kept each other warm.

The night we arrived, I was exhausted and homesick for the familiarity of my house with the blue tile floor, white curtains, my little cat, and even Enrique's predictable grumpiness. I would have been perfectly happy to eat my gallo pinto, take a shower and go to bed while María sat on the porch talking to her mother and stepfather, and TV soap stars wailed over the sound of the rain. But no such luck. It was Friday and I had been pre-selected to accompany 17-year-old Yolanda to participate in a beauty pageant in a muddy little town down the road with a name that means "the near future." Municipal governing bodies make money this way—by hosting pageants where pretty young women collect money from sponsors, and the one who, on pageant night, brings the most money wins the crown. It isn't really about beauty, but being pretty helps.

I couldn't say no. I showered and pulled a crumbled sundress out of my backpack. Someone should have called to tell me to bring something special, but no one had. The red dress in my closet at home would have been perfect, but no one told me I would be accompanying a candidate to a pageant. The evening was interminable. Car rides, hairdos, makeup, and so many dozens of cousins, aunts, friends and friends of friends. My head spun. I wanted a beer. I wanted coffee.

Yolanda was beautiful. She didn't win the pageant, but she was lovely in her shimmering pink gown with flowers in her hair. Boys and men asked her to dance. Some of the bravest ones asked me too, even though my color certainly indicated I might not be the smoothest dancer. They suffered through it politely with me. I missed Enrique's strong grip and forceful step, with which I couldn't possibly go wrong. Dancing with Enrique was holding on for the ride. Everything with Enrique was holding on for the ride.

I ordered myself to enjoy the fiesta. Appreciate it. I would never step foot into this "near future," lost among banana leaves and towering ginger, ever again. Soon—I didn't know how soon—this life would be like a dream. I would be far away from Enrique and his world—a nearly-30-year-old divorcee, trying to get into grad school. I didn't know how it would happen, but it was so close I could taste it. I tried to memorize everything, carve into my heart the sense of belonging, even with family I'd never met in a place I'd never been. I wondered how I would live, afterward. I loved these smelly cantinas with their garish lights, uncomfortable seats, exuberant music, and open hearts. I couldn't imagine how to leave it forever. Forever is a long time.

When it was time for María and me to go home, Enrique drove all the way to the banana plantations to pick us up. He stayed with us for a few days, filling the house with his boisterous joy, loud music, strong cologne, and laugher. He was so beautiful when he pulled into the front yard grinning that I thought maybe—I hoped—maybe, I could find a way to stay with him.

Could I?

Please?

One of us had been angry when I left—I don't remember which one or why—but a week later we weren't angry anymore. María switched beds with me. She slept with Yolanda so that Enrique could sleep with me. The rain on the roof buried all sound.

Part II: Fugitive

A few kilometers down the road I begin flicking glances in the rear view mirror.
What if Enrique goes home for something?
He does that all the time.
He would find my note and know I am leaving.
If he chases me now, he will catch me.
The last time I left him, he chased me all the way to the airport in San José.
And caught me.
I do not want that to happen again.
I was going to pick up my sister, not board a plane, but Enrique didn't know that.
He plead so painfully that I couldn't stand it.
I gave him a second chance.
I review my plan, trying to calm myself.
I see it in my mind on a timeline.
Today I will go to the farm in the mountains north of Liberia.
After I rest for a week where Enrique will not find me, I will drive to San José.

In San José, I have family.
Not blood relatives, adopted family.
The rowdy clan that received me as a student the first time I arrived in Costa Rica as part of a college program has remained connected to me.
Several times a year, I visit them.
I've been to their weddings, their funerals, their baby showers.
Rebeca, the sister who is closest to my age, has visited my home in Los Ríos and met Enrique.
The mother insists that I continue to call her Mami, as her children do.
Rebeca's little daughter calls me Tía.
In San José, I will stay with Mami and sell the truck.
Then, with no truck, I can move around less conspicuously.
I will visit Playa Celeste where, for five years, I have worked.
So many my friends live there.
I will say goodbye to them.
Playa Celeste is only one dangerous hour from Los Ríos, but I will be careful.
Then I will cross Costa Rica's northern border and spend two weeks with David in Nicaragua.
The month of May will begin.
I will come back to the airport in San José, Costa Rica and fly to Atlanta, then.
I am going to get a job in that warm city and earn some money.
I am going to apply to grad school.
I'm smart.
I love school.
I'm going to make something of my life.
Enough of Central America.
Five years is plenty; I've learned what I needed to know.
I am going home.
I am going to be independent, professional, and strong.

No surly husband will shout insults at me, hurt me, frighten me, or forget me on the street corner ever again.

I drive exactly at the posted speed limit because getting stopped by the police could destroy me.
Pulled over by the road, I would be a sitting duck if Enrique is following.
The police would be no help.
I glide through Santa Cruz and keep on toward Liberia.
Liberia is an hour away.
It's a small city, but big enough for a traffic light.
Big enough to swallow me up and make me invisible.
I hope.
I will stop at a supermarket to buy groceries for my days in the mountains.
Vehicles that approach from behind me now or pull up at a crossroads freeze my heart.
Enrique could be anywhere.
I am terrified of every car going any direction.
I have to get to Liberia.

In Liberia, this road crosses the Pan-American highway.
If Enrique is chasing me, he will turn south on that highway toward San José.
He won't imagine where I am going because he has never been to this farm.
Neither have I.
He will think I am driving to the airport like the last time.
Unless, at the intersection, he is so close behind me that he sees me turn the other way.
My imagination torments me with endless terrors.
What if Enrique is there at that intersection after I buy the groceries?

What if he, or someone who knows him, watches the truck turn toward the mountains?
Please God.
I tell myself it won't happen.
I told myself none of this would happen.
I order myself to be calm.
I order myself to think about David.

Enrique took David on as a helper in the pottery workshop, and as a sidekick on his mysterious escapades. They became inseparable—wherever one was, the other couldn't be far. David was Nicaraguan and young, too young to enter a bar in the United States. Maybe Enrique thought David was too young to be dangerous, or young enough to be intimidated. David was dangerous as a hand grenade, and not afraid of the devil.

David moved to Costa Rica with his mother and little sisters years ago when they fled the war that seemed endless, and the arguments with David's step father that seemed endless too. The girls were babies then, and he cared for them while their mother washed clothes and tended other women's children. David fed them, changed their diapers, kept a fire going to heat their milk, and rocked them to sleep. Then, at an age when I was practicing long division, he got a job tending cattle on a ranch to help support the family. And he learned the pottery trade on the side. By the time Enrique pushed me toward him and said "Baile con él," David was living at the pottery workshop, helping the partners with their craft. They called him a "night guard" and let him sleep for free in the corner where Enrique and I had our nest for a time.

Two weeks after Enrique and I returned home from our six months of working in the USA, the yearly Fiestas took place in Santa Cruz. Enrique started it; I didn't, and neither did David. He brought David with us to the Fiestas because he brought David everywhere, bought a round of Coca-Colas outside a discotheque and asked me if I wanted to dance.

I said, "Sí."

"Baile con David," he answered, and pointed at David.

I looked blankly from him to David.

"*Baile,*" Enrique ordered David.

He said he had to drive some people who were going to pay him for a ride. David nodded gravely, pretending to believe him. Enrique said he would be back for me and slipped David money to buy us more sodas. Enrique clearly considered David a safe babysitter for his wife while he went elsewhere with other company. We brought David to the Fiesta that night, and every night after.

There were women. I didn't know who they were. I didn't know where or how many. I only knew I remembered the Enrique who was in love with me, and this was not him. This was someone else. Luckily for me, I was beyond caring.

It was supposed to be innocent because it was Enrique's idea and Enrique was David's benefactor. But it didn't feel innocent. Not when the merengue started, David reached out his hand for me, and what he said with his eyes and his hips as we danced made my cheeks flush. Night after night, Enrique disappeared and David danced with me, getting closer each time, buying me beer instead of sodas which he shouldn't have, leaning in close to me to talk into my ear, putting his hands on me, melting my heart down the insides of my ribcage.

I hadn't wished for any of it. I just wanted to be on the other side of what I knew was coming. Enrique wasn't the new man he'd promised on the lives of his children that he would be when I agreed to give him a second chance. He was the same man as before. I wanted to leave my husband as painlessly as possible and try my life over again far away. I had no interest in vengeance or justice. I had no interest in other men. But into the empty space of pain, anger, and uncertainty came this dazzling smile, these warm arms, these pleading and dangerous eyes. I promised myself to behave honorably. Because Enrique is a cheat doesn't make it right for me to be one. But David wanted everything Enrique scorned. He thought I was brilliant, beautiful, and brave just like Enrique once had.

The Fiestas with their dances ended. I waited for my life to return to normal and find its familiar rhythm. I waited to stop thinking about David. He would be busy working with Enrique and I would be teaching Spanish to foreigners in Playa Celeste. The burning attraction that singed the air between us would cool and soon enough we would smile about the fun we had at the Fiestas. Maybe we would even dance together again someday. I breathed easier, believing I'd escaped unscathed from the danger of terrible temptation.

That isn't what happened. David found excuses almost every day to visit me when Enrique was out of the house. We sat on the front porch so that no one could accuse us of suspicious encounters, and talked for hours. David never ever came inside the house, even for a glass of water, because of the accusations that it could potentially bring. He told me about his childhood during a war I heard about on television while I ate my Captain Crunch before school. His father and three uncles were shot against a wall one morning by the Sandinistas when David was a lump in his mother's belly. The soldiers spared the sister and the youngest brother from their bullets, condemning them to a lifetime of nightmares. David's mother remarried rapidly, as she was unable to provide for her child alone.

I confessed to David that Enrique was unkind to me, that he stormed and shouted and disappeared and there was nothing I could do but watch. I didn't mean to tell him, but he asked. He knew. All of Los Ríos knew. All of Los Ríos knows everything. The town is too small for secrets. I told him I was going to leave. I said I didn't think it would be long.

There were more fiestas in more towns. Enrique packed the double cabin and the bed of our little truck full of friends, I slipped into the passenger seat beside him, and off we went on Saturday nights, Marco Antonio Solís wailing at the top of his lungs from the stereo. David came with us, but we couldn't dance together anymore because Enrique didn't order it. David stayed close, always in the truck cab directly behind me. I felt his gaze, his body heat, the force field that surrounded us burning into my shoulders. When he spoke, the vibration of his voice behind my neck made the hair stand up on my arms and I couldn't breathe.

Then there was the night, late, on the way home from a fiesta somewhere, that Enrique stopped the truck to help the driver of a vehicle stranded along the road. David was the only one in the cab with us that night, and when Enrique closed the door, he was the only one in the cab with me. Night was like a blanket and none of the friends in the truck bed were paying attention. When Enrique stepped away from us, I felt fingers on my arm and turned. David leaned forward and kissed me on the mouth in a hungry way I'd forgotten.

His visits became more daring and more desperate. He tried to convince me not to go, to leave Enrique but to stay in Los Ríos with him instead. I said no. I couldn't. I needed a different life, not a different husband.

He begged. He swore he loved me. Tears came to his eyes and he couldn't speak. I thought of him constantly and wanted every forbidden thing with him, but I could not even pretend to love him. I didn't say I loved him. I loved Enrique. I loved María and Martín, and Enrique's children. And even so, I needed to get out of a ruined marriage and away from a love that was going to destroy me. David said he wanted to be with me forever. I didn't want to think about forever.

But I agreed to see him after I left Enrique. It felt unavoidable. It seemed fair.

A LUCKY BREATH

I park the truck in the alley behind a Liberia supermarket.
I expected to feel safe in Liberia, but I do not.
I feel naked.
I walk into the store, exposed to so many sets of eyes.
I am not supposed to be here.
If I cross someone I recognize now, I must be calm and relaxed.
I concentrate on breathing.
My head spins, and I order myself not to faint.
At the end of each aisle, I turn my cart with dread toward the next, praying to see only strangers.
My heart pounds as if my life is in danger, as if I am being hunted.
I don't know if I am being hunted.
If I find out, it will be too late.

I'd imagined I might buy wine, chocolate—treats to soothe and celebrate.
I don't. I don't want them.
My hands reach for fruits, vegetables, rice, coffee, honey, tea.
Staples will be enough.
I cannot imagine being hungry.

Back in the truck, I slide the directions from my pocket and lay them on the seat beside me.
I am going, now, directly to the farm.
Running away sounds cowardly, but it takes much more courage than I'd imagined.
I pull onto the street and return, trembling, to the traffic light.
I am dying a thousand deaths of terror that there, across the intersection from me, might be Enrique.

He isn't there.

The light changes and I turn right, heading north toward the mountains, toward the farm, toward freedom.

When I leave the highway 15 minutes later, what begins as a paved road degenerates into a jumble of rocks.

I've seen bad roads in rural areas, but I have never seen anything like this.

My little truck climbs up and up in first and second gear, barely clearing the boulders from which the road is made.

Eventually, no more cars come down the mountain toward me. Soon, there are no more houses.

I am alone in virgin forest, laboring over impossible stones.

The mountain grows larger and larger, the way steeper, the scenery more breathtaking.

I have the sensation of crawling to safety, of wiggling into a hiding place.

Enrique will never find me here.

He doesn't know about the farm and has never seen this road.

He would never imagine that I would have the courage to travel alone this far into nothing.

I fear I have missed a turn somewhere.

I realize I will be stranded if the road worsens even a little bit.

There are no other travelers.

A LUCKY BREATH

Enrique's second son Miguel loved school. He especially loved learning to write. He spread his first grade notebooks on my kitchen table in the afternoons to practice carving the shapes of letters and making words. He filled page after page with laboriously-crafted capitals spelling each of our names, repeating them with comic seriousness. He looked like a Mini Enrique with his deep brown puppy eyes and walnut skin. Adán, a few years older and not a fan of sitting still, didn't like school. He laughed at Miguel painstakingly writing Diana Enrique Diana Enrique across the page, line after line. He preferred to throw rocks at iguanas and climb jocote trees the minute he kicked off his uniform and shoes.

Carina María, almost old enough for kindergarten, said she wanted to be a teacher like me. I bought her a preschool workbook of pre-writing exercises so she could join us at the table on hot afternoons in front of the fan, tracing curley-q's, slashes, and connecting the dots. I pushed aside my journals and the pages of what I hoped might be a book someday to supervise Miguel's letters and Carina's symbols.

In my moments of heartbreak and rage at Enrique, I wanted to walk out the door and never come back. But then I would find myself sitting at the table with these grimy wiggly little ones so diligently forcing their pencils to make letters because they wanted to be like me. And then I couldn't bear to think of walking away. No one else would sit with Carina and Miguel, pointing out what was right about their efforts, not what was wrong. Would they grow up to hate me for leaving them? Would they call me a liar? Would I be just a crazy gringa who came to them and then left them for something easier? Would they even remember me? When they had children, someday, would I even know? Torturous questions circled my brain.

But I couldn't stand the idea of being, for them, one more example of a woman accepting mistreatment and disrespect from her husband. They had plenty of examples of that around them. Someone, even if it was only one person, ever, needed to model self-love to these three sets of adoring eyes. If not me, then who? Who else would provide Carina María with proof that she could choose whatever kind of life she wanted to live? What good would it be for a broken stepmother to speak to her someday of agency and self-respect? Who else would demonstrate to little Adán and Miguel that a wife will not always acquiesce? I hoped to give them so much more than letters.

I sensed that our time was growing short, although I didn't know how short. I wanted my children to remember me. I wanted Miguel to love school even if he grew up not to love me, and for Carina María to be a teacher. It's not that I thought a few afternoons at the table with me would make a significant difference. But when they came to me with their books and pencils, saying, "Enséñame," I took the chance to draw them in.

A LUCKY BREATH

Finally, I see a fence.
The forest gives way to a corral.
A house comes into view and a second house after it.
Beyond this is nothing but mountain terrain.
I stop.
This must be the farm.
I may not be brave enough to continue if it isn't.
A man rides up to me on a horse and smiles curiously.
I mention my friend's name and ask if this is the farm that belongs to her.
He says yes.
He points me to the large house.
He and explains that he is the farm's employee and that he and his family live in the little house across the creek.

I park the truck under a giant mango tree that overshadows the front yard and try the key in the front door.
The lock releases.
I have made it to safety.
Escaped.
Run away.
Vanished into thin air.
It is mid-morning of the same day on which I woke in the dark and lay beside Enrique listening to roosters.

I carry everything I have left of my life inside the spacious farmhouse I'm going to live in for five days.
The house is encircled by a wide porch, has a perfect kitchen, large sunny windows, and a living room with a telephone.
The year is 2000, and telephones in remote areas of Costa Rica are rare.

Cell phones are a thing we've seen in movies.

Although I am safe here, my fear does not loosen its grip.
My heart pounds.
Each noise—gusts of wind, the footfalls of a horse, human voices, anything that breaks the silence—shoots a wave of terror through me.
Can Enrique be coming after me?
Could he describe the truck, ask around, find me?
Inside of me, I can't find the peace that lies all around me.
I didn't expect this constant, nauseating fear.
Hiding is not fun when it isn't a game.
I have never been hunted.
I feel hunted now.
I give in to my pounding heart and move the truck behind the house.
I park it, absurdly, in the middle of the back yard where it is not visible from the road that has no travelers.
Reason insists there is no way Enrique will find me here, but I am frightened.
I am a fugitive.
When the truck is behind the house, I relax.
I stop tensing at every sound.
The beauty of the mountain farm begins to dawn on me.

A LUCKY BREATH

Enrique's second chance would never have lasted an entire year if we hadn't spent most of it in the United States. When he broke the windows and I drove away in the thunderstorm, we'd already purchased our tickets. We were leaving in a month.

My sister Kelly's in-laws own a fruit farm in Washington State, and they'd agreed to hire Enrique and me as seasonal workers. It would be grueling work for minimum wage, but it was so much more than we earned in Costa Rica. We sold our little car so that when we came back with our pockets full of money, we could buy a pickup truck. My parents signed the sponsorship papers enabling Enrique to apply for a green card. Maybe, if things went well, we could work the harvest season every year. I hoped this experience would save us. I hoped that during our eight months in the USA something would happen that would make everything be ok, that would keep this brilliant love from ending in fire and smoke.

Maybe living in the USA could somehow change Enrique, make him understand me by understanding the world I came from. Maybe if he saw a new way of life and experienced examples of marriages that were not like ours? Maybe he would see that not all men cheat on their wives, shout at them, and disregard their feelings? It couldn't hurt. I just hoped for a miracle, and I didn't care what form it took. I didn't have a specific thing I wanted to happen other than our marriage not to be smashed like the pottery and the bathroom door.

Enrique and I worked with Mexican immigrants in the orchards from May until December. In the chilly days of May, we thinned apples. In the warm days of June, we harvested sweet cherries. Through the scalding month of July, we harvested sour cherries. In the unmerciful heat of August, we grafted infant apple trees in the hot dust. As schools opened in September, we tied apple branches to trellises. On chilly October mornings, we waited for sunrise to begin the apple harvest. Bundled up to our eyes in November and December, we trudged through the orchards with pruning shears in our gloved hands. We shared my sister Kelly and her husband's home, drove a car that belonged to the farm, and saved most of our income.

Enrique controlled his rages and didn't disappear with the car because he couldn't. But being immersed in American culture didn't make him want to be a new man; it made me want to be a new woman.

I admitted to myself that my life with Enrique wasn't a place that I would want to raise children. I would never want them to witness the disrespect I accepted from him. I realized the sweet moments that made me fall in love with Enrique, the good times when we were so happy, happened years ago. All of them. I could never be 100% certain, on any given day, that he wouldn't break sobriety again. And if he got drunk enough, I knew what he could do. I could never be sure that he would come home. The pain of that crippled me. If I were alone, I would not be lonelier, sadder, or more disappointed than I was with Enrique. And at least on my own, no one would shout at me or insult me. And the only thing I could do about any of it was to walk away.

I didn't have a new plan; I just recognized the current one was broken. Of course, I wouldn't desert Enrique while we were in a foreign country; that seemed unnecessarily cruel. He didn't even speak English. No reason to be overly dramatic. I wanted to go home to my life in Los Ríos, my house, the warm ocean, and the children. I loved Enrique even though that love was hurting me. There would be plenty of time later to work out what to do.

The cherry harvest came and went. Apple harvest came in the fall, then pruning season, as winter arrived. I snapped my pruning shears at the branches and thought about grad school. In the evenings while Enrique watched television in the living room, I talked to Kelly about my thoughts in the kitchen over tea and cookies. Upstairs in the cold little bedroom under the covers, I lay still as death beside Enrique and hoped he wouldn't reach for me. He seldom did. I promised myself to start separating, to begin getting used to it, not to fall prey to that circle of warmth that emanated from him. An unwelcome embrace from me might land an elbow in my belly or a heel on my shin bone. No more, I told myself. Not ever. And never once, after I stopped sliding my arm around him in the night, did he ask me why or what was wrong.

I kept these thoughts to myself so that we could return to our home and family together. I knew that when the moment came, I would take the next step. It would come. I was sure I would recognize it. It wouldn't be easy, but it wouldn't be harder than living like this for the rest of my life.

We left the USA for Costa Rica at the end of December 1999. The entire Campos family, complete with in-laws, nieces, nephews, and Enrique's parents met us at the airport in San José. My heart burst into a thousand pieces, and I prayed that Enrique would be perfect. I didn't want to leave him. I didn't want to leave them. I didn't want to leave us. I loved my house, my life, and my family.

We bought a little gray pick-up truck which I insisted be registered in my name. The house was in Enrique's name, so the truck should be in mine, I said. And we went back to the little house I'd expected to live in forever. But I didn't expect that anymore.

Angel calls me on the phone the first night.
He asks how I am.
I tell him I am alright.
He tells me that they miss me.
I try not to start crying.
He tells me that Enrique didn't return to the house and find the note until six in the evening.
My premonitions of being followed were all false.
Angel tells me that Enrique is in a rage, saying that starting tomorrow he will look for me everywhere until he finds me.
He won't find me.
I tell Angel it is impossible.
I promise him Enrique will not find me no matter how hard he tries.
I say I am safe, and that a kind family lives nearby.
And I anxiously wait for the other phone call I expect—the one from David.

Mornings on the mountain are cold.
I make hot coffee and sip it in my sweatshirt, curled on the chair on the chilly porch.
In the solitude of that farmhouse, I try to remember how to breathe.
I listen to birds calling through the mountains and think of Enrique.
How he loved loud music and the television, and had no time for birds.
I remembered us before the truck, before the television, when all we had was the radio on the windowsill in our bedroom in Santa Cruz.

We were happy, then.
I cry.
I wander to the kitchen for more coffee.
I pick a book and read for a while until the sun has warmed the air.

The days at the mountain farm pass sweetly, and sadly.
I am never bored and I am no longer afraid.
I am not lonely.
The aloneness that is around me, I have chosen.
It is the medicine that will heal me when I have taken enough of it.
I climb trees and go for morning walks and afternoon jogs.
The children of the family next door take me on horseback rides through wooded ravines and over breathtaking hillsides.
I turn on the antiquated TV set, but the sound of it makes me sad, so I turn it off again.
I talk to myself, to God, to the angels.
I wash my clothes, make more coffee, slice mangos and pineapples, open my suitcases and look at my things.
I take them out and spread them on the floor—what is left of my life.
I had a house, a home, a husband, and children.
Now I have a suitcase of clothing, books, and pictures.
Everything old is gone and everything new is still waiting to arrive.

I open my journals and read about Enrique, about the good days and bad days.
There were so many days.
I laugh out loud.
I cry lying on the floor among my own words.
I climb hills and gaze down over valleys, knowing that I am at

a place I have always been going.
I know that horribly painful and difficult things lay ahead, but others already lay behind.
I sleep deeply and struggle with Enrique in my dreams.

David calls me on most of my five nights in the mountains.
David says Enrique follows him.
He tells me that Enrique suspects he knows where I am, so he keeps the phone number hidden in his shoe.
David has no idea where I am, but keeping the paper with that number is dangerous for him.
We talk about our trip to Nicaragua.
He tells me about the dances he will take me to and the beaches where we will walk.
Angel and David report to me about Enrique.
He wants to search for me, they say, but doesn't know where to begin.
He waits for me to return.
He alternates between fury and grief, they say.
I am familiar with both of these emotions.
Day after day, Enrique refuses to eat.
Later, when I do not return, he refuses to leave the house.
I write him a letter with no return address, saying I'm sorry for the way I left, but that he should not look for me or wait for me to come home.
I will mail it from San José.

I dressed as fast as I could because I didn't know when Enrique would be back. I was scared. He would be back for the car keys sooner or later, even drunker than before, and I didn't plan to find out what he would do to get them. I knew very well Enrique could break my neck. I wanted to collapse on the bed and cry my eyes out about everything that was destroyed, but I didn't have time.

Still shaking, I walked to the safety of María's house. I ate a few bites of rice and beans with Enrique's mortified family while the thunderstorm blew in from the east. Sudden wind howled. Enrique returned home from the cantina. From where I sat at María's table, I listened to him shouting and things crashing inside our house as he ransacked it for the keys. He didn't find them. He didn't dare come into his parents' house looking for me. Enrique raged. Lightning flashed closer and closer.

We watched, in the wild wind before the first drops of rain hit, as Enrique stumbled out of our house, through his parents' yard, and continued on to the house on the opposite side of the yard where his ex, Inez, lived with the children. There, he laid down outside the front door and fell into a drunken sleep. Thunder slammed through the sky, and fat raindrops splattered the dust. The electricity flickered and failed, draping a blanket of black over Los Ríos.

There was no way in the world I was going to lie in my own bed that night, in my destroyed house waiting to see what Enrique would do when he came back. I told Enrique's family I was going to leave for three or four days. I told them I'd be alright.

They said that was a good decision. They agreed I should leave and let Enrique think about what he'd done. Don't come back to him, they said. Make him come to you.

I ran through the lightning and rain to the ruin of my house.

The deafening sound of water hammered the roof and bright flashes split the sky like a scene from a movie as I crunched, crying, over the broken glass in my bedroom. Rain and wind whipped the white curtains at the open windows while I jammed mismatched clothes into a backpack by the beam of a flashlight, sobbing. Leaving. Running away like a thief. From my own house. From my life I fought so hard for. But how could I lie down in that bed and sleep with shattered glass all around me? What if Enrique came back in a few minutes or hours and demanded the keys? What if he hurt me? He didn't deserve the keys and he didn't deserve me. He didn't deserve a pretty house with windows to break. He deserved to wake up in the morning with a terrible hangover, no money, no wife, and broken everything. The rest, we could sort out later. I could not possibly shout loud enough to tell him how not ok any of this was.

I didn't expect I was leaving forever, but I knew I needed to get out immediately and not come back until something happened. I didn't know what it would be. I got in the car with my backpack and drove through the storm back to Playa Celeste, wondering where to go.

It was not a pleasant surprise for my friends in Playa Celeste when I pulled up late at night with puffy eyes asking to stay with them. They hesitated. They didn't want a scene with Enrique, they said. What if he came looking for me? I promised I had told no one where I was going, and that I would leave in the morning, if they wanted. They gave in and let me have the extra bed.

My sister Michelle made an emergency visit to keep me from going back to Enrique, which I did anyway because he was my husband. I loved him. On the way to pick her up at the airport in San José, I drove through Los Ríos, and stopped to see María. Because I couldn't call her on the telephone, this was the only way to tell her I was alright and that my sister was coming to keep me company. I hoped I wouldn't have to face Enrique, and I didn't. As usual, Enrique was out.

Traffic on the Pan-American Highway was light that day and I arrived at the airport in only four hours. I was sitting under a tree outside the terminal writing in my journal when I looked up and saw Enrique walking across the grass toward me. He startled me almost out of my mind.

He was disheveled and hadn't eaten in days. He trembled and nearly wept. When he'd heard I had come through Los Ríos on my way to the airport, he'd thought I was leaving the country. He'd run to Mateo's house and pleaded with him to catch me before I got on the plane. They chased me down on Mateo's motorcycle.

Enrique sank to the ground beside me. He begged me to forgive him and come back home. He said he couldn't live without me. He swore he couldn't live without me. He promised never ever to drink, ever again. He promised on the lives of his mother and his children to be a different man, a kind husband, anything I wanted. What I wanted was to believe him.

I decided to give him a second chance. Just one. Not because I believed he could do it. But because I loved him, and I wanted him to be the person he was describing. If he could be a new man, I wanted to know it. If he couldn't, I wanted to know that too.

The five days I have at the farm are over too fast.
It's time to take the next step.
I must leave my hiding place.
Now, I must drive to San José to sell the truck.
To do this I will pass through Liberia again.
The thought frightens me as much now as it did five days ago.
Liberia is terribly close to home.
Someone could see me.
And tell Enrique.
But I have no other choice.
There is only one way to San José from here.
I will be in good company in San José, safe, and very well fed.
All I must do is arrive unseen.
That, and navigate the truck through the incomprehensible snarl of streets that twists through the city.
I've been there dozens of times, but always on the bus.

I pack the truck and drive down from the mountains while the morning is still cool.
I start early because the journey will be long.
Protests are taking place across the country.
I've seen it on the news on the ancient little TV.
The government intends to privatize the country's only electric utility company, and opponents of the plan have taken to the streets.
Citizens are blocking the highways with tires, barrels, and their own bodies.
A trip that should take three hours will probably take all day.
Just after the rocky road turns to pavement, traffic stops.
Protesters block the highway even before I arrive in Liberia.

My body bursts into a cold sweat.
I remind myself that if anyone in this line of vehicles recognizes me, it will be hours until they can tell Enrique.
They will be stuck in the same line of traffic as I am.
Traffic flow resumes.
An hour later, as I approach the next city, more protesters block the road.
People step out of their cars to buy food, use public telephones and restrooms, chat, and shake their heads.
Along the entire length of the Pan-American highway, traffic stops at barricades, resumes when police officers arrive to remove obstacles, and stops again at the next block.
I am a white fugitive in a country of brown faces.
It is impossible for me to hide or to remain inconspicuous.
I pull my baseball cap low and keep my gaze down, but the color of my skin is loud.

At roadblock after roadblock, cars stop, engines idle, and drivers roll down the windows hoping for a breeze.
The farther I am from the home I no longer have, the more I am able to relax and appreciate this peaceful protest.
No one shouts, curses, or blows the horn.
Vendors amble along the stopped cars selling empanadas, platanos fritos, salted green mangos and cold drinks.
Delayed drivers turn their radios loud, giving lines of traffic the beat of an impromptu street party.
We are all going to be late, but no one is getting hurt.

After 10 hours, I reach the outskirts of San José.
I am exhausted.
It is dark, and I can't bear to imagine deciphering the city streets tonight.

I find a hotel with a secure parking lot where I won't have to unload my heavy boxes from the truck.

From the phone in my room, I call Mami and tell her I'll be there tomorrow.

I sleep poorly, wake early, and arrive in San José the next morning.

I left Enrique twice, but I only went back once. The first time, I left because I was afraid.

It happened at the end of Easter Week, six months after we moved into our new house beside María and Martín. During the holidays, all the brothers and their families who live in the city take the bus to Los Ríos to spend their vacation together. It's a tradition. María and Martín's house fills to bursting with brothers, sisters-in-law, and babies. Cousins carouse with the chickens and dogs, and every day is laundry day. The cooking fire in the outdoor kitchen never goes out. Someone is always brewing a pot of coffee, patting out tortillas, stirring up a syrupy pudding made from tree-ripened fruit and sugar cane, or plotting which chicken's neck to wring in the morning. The town's water supply invariably runs short with the influx of extended family in every house, so water is rationed and bucket baths are the order of the day. I loved it.

Enrique hated it. It made him grumpier than ever and meaner than usual. Anything not orchestrated by him infuriated Enrique. He hated having his routine of disappearances disturbed. There were more people than usual to ask him questions about where he was going and why he was never home. Enrique spent Easter Week scowling, making excuses, working long hours at the pottery shop even though it was supposedly closed, and driving around in the car with his sunglasses on and the music turned loud.

The family couldn't help but notice. One by one, the brothers and sisters-in-law pulled me aside to quietly ask me how Enrique was treating me. I said he was alright. It was a lie, but I was ashamed of what I allowed. I could have left him, but I didn't. They asked me if he was drinking. I said no. He wasn't. Except for the slip-up on the night he forgot me in Santa Cruz, Enrique hadn't had a drink in almost a year. I didn't mention that incident to them. I didn't want to talk about it. He's just like that, I said. I don't know why. Don't worry about me. I'm okay.

The Saturday before Easter Sunday you go to the beach. Everyone in Los Ríos goes to the beach. Everyone in the province of Guanacaste goes to the beach. The Campos brothers all pitched in and hired a van with a driver to take the whole family to Playa Celeste for the day. I offered our car as well, saying that Enrique and I could take some of the kids.

When I told Enrique that I'd volunteered to drive to the beach, he was furious. He roared he wasn't going to the beach, that he didn't like the beach, and that he had to work. But no one works on Easter Saturday. I knew what he wanted. He wanted the car. I don't know where he wanted to go, and I wasn't supposed to know. But this time I wasn't giving in. I said if he decided to stay home, I was still going with his family, and still taking the car. Our kids and a few cousins would ride with me. Then he was even angrier, but what could he say? It was his family. They knew it was my car.

It was a hot, sunny day at the beach. I splashed in the shallows with the kids, and at noon, ate a plate of the arroz con pollo María made for the occasion. In the afternoon, Martín and I walked the long beach. I noted the dark clouds piling up on the horizon to the east and hoped they would stay there, inland. Martín said he wished Enrique was with us. He said he was sorry Enrique was so quarrelsome and mean. I said I wished too that Enrique was here, and that he was happy. I said I didn't know why he wasn't. An ominous feeling crept over me as the afternoon deepened and storm clouds billowed blacker over the hills. I hoped it was unfounded anxiety, not a premonition.

It was not unfounded anxiety; it was a premonition. At that moment, Enrique was in the cantina with his friend Alejandro where they were drinking themselves into complete oblivion.

When I arrived home just before dark with my sandy cargo of cousins, Enrique was stumbling around the front porch of our house smashing the pottery he made, smashing windows, and trying to kick in the door. He was insanely drunk, both boisterous and vicious in a way that I recognized from the night he pulled my hair.

I was scared. I tried not to show it to the kids, but I was. Alejandro stood watching Enrique in bleary helplessness, saying nothing. Across the yard, the van was pulling up to María's house and everyone could see the disaster unfolding in front of me. I sent the kids hurrying to join the rest of the family and I opened the door with my key before Enrique broke it down. He followed me inside.

I knew what was going to happen next. Enrique was going to want the car keys and so help me, I wasn't going to give them up. He would destroy the car, himself, and who knows what else if I did. I knew it was going to be rough. I needed a plan and I didn't have one.

I said I wanted to take a shower, and locked myself in the bathroom without a single comment to Enrique about his drunkenness or the broken pieces of things everywhere. I wanted none of that blind fury directed at me. I looked desperately around the bathroom for a place to hide the keys and I found it. The sound of the shower covered me as I lifted the lid of the toilet tank and placed the car keys in the water. He would never think to look there. And now I had to get to María's house as quickly as possible. Who knew what Enrique would do in this condition to get the keys from me? Look what he had done to the windows.

As I rinsed the salt and sand from my body, Enrique slammed the door with his fist, shouting, "Dame las llaves!"

"Un momento!" I called back.

A blast to the door must have been a body slam. "Dame las llaves!" he roared.

"Un momento," I called again. "Me estoy bañando." This was getting uglier than I thought, and faster. Enrique screamed again for the keys and slammed the door. I understood that I should have gone straight to María's house but it was too late now. I turned the water off and reached for the towel.

Two kicks to the bathroom door from Enrique's booted foot and the screws that held the hinges tore free. I barely had time to wrap the towel around me before Enrique yanked me, naked and wet, out of the bathroom. Alejandro looked away. Enrique pushed me against the doorway and shouted that this is his house and he wants the keys. The door frame dug into my back and his fingers were hurting my arm.

Alejandro stepped in for me, then. "Cálmese," he ordered Enrique. "Déjela. Pobrecita. No hagas eso."

Enrique shouted something unintelligible at Alejandro and pushed me again.

"Vamos a la cantina," Alejandro ordered. "Vamos a tomar una cerveza. Déjela."

And just like that, Enrique forgot about the keys. He turned and followed Alejandro out of the house toward the cantina.

Adán and Miguel appeared in the doorway, wide-eyed with curiosity and horror. They'd seen their daddy drunk before, but never smashing doors and windows. Never screaming at me. I tried not to cry in front of them, to find another way through my fear and my fury. Adán, brave and protective at eleven years old, walked carefully through the splintered glass on the floor and put his arms around me where I stood by the broken bathroom door, stunned, in my towel. "No llore, Diana," he said while he hugged me. "Mañana mi papá va a estar mejor y se lo va a limpiar todo."

"Sí, lo sé," I said, crying anyway, but not about the shattered glass or the broken door. He thought I was crying about the windows and the pottery—about the mess. The mess I was crying about didn't have a way to be cleaned up.

A LUCKY BREATH

I drive straight from the hotel to the same dealership where, three months ago, Enrique and I bought the truck.
Selling it isn't as easy as I think it will be, and they don't offer the price I wanted.
They offer a terrible price, a fraction of what we paid for it.
What was I thinking?
Anyone who drives a truck loaded with luggage into a dealership and says, "I need to sell this," isn't going to get a good price.
I should have known better.
I try not to look desperate, trapped.
They offer me one million colones.
One million is a big number but the colon is small currency.
That amount is nothing.
Stupidly and to my utter embarrassment, I start to cry.
I cry with disappointment about the terrible price and, having started with that, about everything else.
I can't stop crying.
None of this is what I wanted.
I cry because I want to keep the truck and go home.
I cry because I will never go home, ever.
I cry because in my mind Enrique screams at me:
"Lo vendiste por solo un millón de colones?!
Que idiota que eres!
Que tonta!
Qué estabas pensando?"
Everyone at the car dealership is embarrassed.
I am embarrassed too.
They try to be kind to me, but I know they can't wait for me to leave.

Neither can I.
Tears stream from my eyes as I sign the papers.
I need to blow my nose.
Finally, it's done.
The confused car dealer flags me a taxi and helps me load my bags and boxes into it.
I ride through the city's twisted streets up to the section named Guadalupe where Mami lives.
This is my second home.
We haul my mountain of things out of the taxi and push them into a corner in the home's small dining room.
In this compact city home, the pile looks enormous.
They know I have left my home, but even so, everyone asks why I have so many things.
I do not know what to say.
This is nothing.
I had a house with a blue floor and white curtains, a little cat, a washing machine, and a room with a desk.
Why do I look like I've been crying, they wonder?
Is Enrique looking for me?
Have I talked to him?
How much money did I get for the truck?
I spend the night.
After five days of solitude at the farm, it is good to be among people again.
Loving people.
After five days of solitude at the farm, I long for five more.

The next day, I visit Lenny and his family who live across the valley on the other side of the city.
Their baby, a beautiful wild-haired little girl named Veronica, was to be my goddaughter.
Now we will be strangers.

When I say goodbye to them, they cry.
Even baby Veronica cries.
I stand there heartbroken and stupidly dry-eyed.
I am too destroyed even for tears.

I go back to Mami's home in Guadeloupe.
Mami makes coffee and spreads cookies, bread, and slices of ham and cheese on the table.
Rebeca comes with her little girl and we have coffee.
The toddler makes us laugh.
I wish I could stay here.
I pretend I am still an exchange student, the eager stumbling pup we all remember me as, that Rebeca still lives here, and that tonight we will steal Papi's rum again and giggle ourselves to sleep in the little room at the top of the stairs.
Just one more time.
Just one.

I pack a backpack.
I'm going to Playa Celeste in the morning to see friends and say goodbye to them.
Traveling will be easier, now.
I can disappear into any corner.
Playa Celeste is a dangerous choice for me.
It is close to Los Ríos and is the first place Enrique would look for me, but I've been gone for almost two weeks and Enrique isn't looking in the first place anymore.
I hear he isn't looking anywhere.
Angel says he isn't leaving the house and still isn't eating.
Besides, even if Enrique hears I am in Playa Celeste and comes for me, it doesn't matter.
I won't be alone.
Plenty of people will surround me.

He wouldn't dare to hurt me.

I wouldn't dare to change my mind.

It's too late for him to take the truck away.

From Playa Celeste, a bus will take me to Liberia where I will meet David and we will visit Nicaragua.

In a few weeks, all of this will be over and I will be on a plane to Atlanta.

A LUCKY BREATH

Sitting in the rocking chairs on his front porch, Martín and I had long lazy Sunday afternoon talks. María would be busy in the kitchen. The children would be off somewhere picking papapturros and slapping at weeds with sticks they pretend are machetes. Enrique, of course, was always elsewhere. I would think of a pretext to wander through the yard, hoping to find Martín there lost in reverie. He would invite me to sit. We spent hours trying to imagine each other's lives, pondering each other's equally strange stories and feeding a deep affection that filled in the spaces between us.

Martín would turn to me, his daughter-in-law from another planet, and start by saying, "…Yo me pregunto…" then tell me what it is he wondered. All of his questions were personal. About what it is that drew me to Los Ríos. About my parents. About whether or not I thought I might someday move back to the United States. He could understand leaving home to look for a better life, like he had done when he went to work in the Caribbean banana plantations and came back with a wife and money to buy a farm, but he couldn't understand me.

I didn't have a lot to say for myself. I hadn't come to look for a better life, and by many standards the life I left was "better" than this one. But not by mine.

Martín didn't question me out of a burning need to understand; he loved to converse. So, we conversed. Sometimes I managed to turn the conversation around, and instead of trying to find words to explain what someone like me was doing in his world and in his family, I listened to him tell stories. About the banana plantations. About meeting María. About Los Ríos in the time of a dozen houses and no running water. About the day Los Ríos' wealthiest family got electricity and how everyone gathered in the shadows outside their windows at night, elbowing each other for a *glimpse of the flickering black and white television screen.* He told me about the time they found baby Enrique crawling toward a fat curled rattlesnake, enthralled by the warning sound of the tail. They couldn't run to him. They had to call and cajole him until he turned, smiling, and crawled the other way. The snake, disconcerted but unthreatened by the child, warned but did not strike.

María sometimes brought us coffee and sweet bread. Martín and I rocked. I told him about airplane rides, snow, ice skating, and the thousands of chickens on my parents' farm. They were beautiful hours. "Pongamos…" Martín would say, looking off into the distance, and then repeat back to me what I was explaining to him to see if he had it right.

María told me that Enrique was just like his father—that Martín drank guaro in the cantinas, shouted about everything, and had other women when he was young. I looked at this gentle old man on the rocking chair next to me. He absentmindedly scolded Adán and Miguel for pestering the dog and poked affectionate fun at María for her sweet tooth. He carried buckets of water to his two cows twice a day and loved to spray the veranera with the hose in the dry season, but mostly Martín sat and rocked. It was impossible to imagine him acting like Enrique. But I knew María wouldn't say it if it wasn't true.

I tried to imagine Enrique as a docile old man sitting on the porch sweetly teasing me and getting up to come to the table to eat when he was called. I wondered how long I would have to wait for that. Forty years? Was it worth it? Was it even possible? What kind of thing is that to live for?

I rocked and smiled at Martín. *La Esperanza es lo último que se pierde,* they say. Hope is the last thing you lose. I still had some. I planned to make it last as long as I could. If for nothing else, for more moments like these.

A LUCKY BREATH

At the beach in Playa Celeste, I am almost happy.
For three days, I am on vacation in the place I've worked for years.
I've earned it.
My friends make room for me in their extra bedrooms and on their couches.
I swim in their pools, tell them about my exodus from Los Ríos, and drink rum punches.
I tell about how I ran away from my home and hid in the mountains.
I give back the keys to the farmhouse, unable to express the depth of my gratitude.
I wander the pristine stretches of familiar beach I have come to love over these five years.
I sink into the warm water like an embrace.
My throat aches.
I don't want to leave Costa Rica.
I chose it for my life.
I don't want to go away, defeated.
Neither do I want to stay and continue this losing battle to be happy with Enrique.
I miss my little house, the room I had with a writing desk, and my little cat.
I hope Enrique doesn't hurt him.
I hope he is being fed.

In the evenings, I borrow a bicycle and ride around town.
I feel so free, I can almost fly.
I am so light I think I will float away into the sky like a balloon.
I try to remember how to be one person.

I practice being only me, not us.
It is so easy and so hard.

On the third evening, David calls.
The next morning, I will meet him at the bus station in Liberia.
It's a busy station with buses from all over the country.
I tell myself no one in it will know me.
And even if someone does, Enrique would never be able to catch up with me if he tried.
By the time he got there, I would be in Nicaragua.

I should get on a plane, not on a bus to the border.
Something tells me this but I do not want to listen.
Everything is done and it is time for me to leave.
But I don't want to go.
I know this will make leaving even harder but I don't care.
I am tired of being good, of being right, of being strong.
I want to go far away, lie my head on David's shoulder, stop fighting, stop trying, and let everything happen.
Float.
I have suffered so much already that I don't care if I suffer more.
In the end, there will be nothing.
I am not afraid of it.

The car was alright except for a dent and a broken headlight. Enrique got out, tired and bleary but unscathed. I stood in the kitchen holding my coffee and stared at him as if he were a stranger as he entered the house.

"No me digas nada," he said, and stumbled a little. He sank wearily on the couch.

"Dónde estaba?" I asked.

"Ningún lado," he answered.

I repeated the question.

"Me fui para Nicoya," he said.

"A hacer qué?" I asked.

"Nada," he said. "No me diga nada. Quiero dormir." He got up, went into the bathroom, and turned on the shower.

He wasn't getting off with that. Later, when he was lying on the bed, I walked into our room and lay down beside him. My stomach churned with fury, relief, and the exhaustion of a night spent listening for him to return and hearing every sound in Los Ríos.

I asked him if he'd been drinking even though it was obvious that he had. He didn't lie.

I asked him what happened to the car.

He said it hit a wall.

I asked him who he was with.

He called me stupid.

I asked him who he was with.

He said no one.

I said I didn't believe him. Then said he'd gone to give money to Sandrita. She'd sent word that she needed money for Melani, the baby. Money for milk and diapers. For a doctor. And he felt sorry for her. That's what he said. Nothing happened, he said. Nothing except that while I was teaching, he went to Nicoya to give his money to Sandrita for her baby, and he didn't come home until the next day.

I imagined the three of them together and the knot in my stomach almost made me vomit. Even if the baby wasn't his—if she was Angel's, and by now I realized she probably wasn't—she was family either way. It's not the baby's fault she never should have been conceived.

I told him I waited for him after class in Santa Cruz from 4:30 in the afternoon until 9:00. On the street corner with my books and my pretty dress.

He said I should have taken a taxi and called me stupid.

I said I did take a taxi. And I am not stupid. Although at the moment I didn't feel I could prove it.

Enrique slept for three hours, and I slept too, finally. When he woke, he put on his best shirt, doused himself in cologne, and told me to get dressed. He was sober now, sheepish, and almost kind. I asked where we were going. He said again to get dressed. He said he didn't know.

We drove to Santa Cruz and ate lunch in a restaurant. I was quiet. He was quiet. I knew in this culture men didn't apologize to women. I knew he felt me requiring an apology, and this was it. Enrique never had words for apologies. They floated in the air, but they never materialized. Enrique, when he apologized, did it with money—by telling me to get dressed, putting gas in the car, and buying meals neither of us could do more than taste no matter how hungry we were.

Enrique drove all day, trying to run away from himself. He played loud music and we didn't talk much. We drove north until we got to the border of Nicaragua. Then we turned around and drove back. We ate ice cream, walked on beaches, and Enrique bought me a pretty necklace. We drove until dark. I don't know what he was thinking about.

I know what I was thinking about. I was thinking, this is not my life. I am 28 years old and this is not my life.

Everything inside me was broken. He left me standing on the street corner and didn't come home. My husband. What do you do when this happens? What's the right thing? His culture explains it away, saying, "Ojos que no ven, corazón que no siente," but that is a lie. My heart was in a thousand pieces.

I arrive at the bus station in Liberia before noon.
The noisy, dirty terminal connects this cowboy town with the outside world.
I don't know how long I will wait for David, or which bus will bring him.
San José?
Santa Cruz?
Flamingo?
Nicoya?
It doesn't matter.
I will wait all day for him if I have to.
I fear that at any moment, I could find myself face to face with someone who recognizes me, so I sit as far as possible from the milieu.
I'm used to it by now.
Everywhere I go, I scan the perimeter for the least conspicuous spots.
I pick a restaurant in the back corner of the terminal and sit at a table by the kitchen.
A claw crane game full of stuffed animals hides me from view.
I can lean forward to watch buses unload, then discreetly sip café con leche while I wait.

My relationship with Enrique is over.
But my relationship with Enrique's family isn't.
That relationship will be ruined if I am caught with another man.
Especially this man.
Costa Ricans look down on Nicaraguans, their longsuffering and less affluent neighbors to the north.

Based on nothing more than our birthplaces, no one would think David is good enough for me.
Enrique's family supports my decision to leave him because they agree the way he treated me was unfair.
If they find out what I am doing now, their affection for me will be destroyed.
There will be no forgiveness.
It would be a terrible slap in the face for them.
To land a slap in Enrique's face would be a pleasure, but María and Martín, no.
I cannot bear to imagine.
They will assume I have been unfaithful.
I haven't.
With David, I am hiding not only from my husband.
I am hiding from everyone.

Eventually, the face I am waiting for appears in the stream of so many faces.
David is here.
His eyes skim the perimeter where he expects I will be and he spots me when I move.
Already, I've forgotten how beautiful he is.
We embrace nervously and he sits with me.
I order him a coffee while we wait for our bus.
He tells me how he left Los Rios this morning, how Enrique came to the workshop just as he was shouldering his heavy pack and asked where he was going.
My heart clenches and forgets to release.
David laughs a little and says he told Enrique he was going to Nicoya to sell a few pieces of pottery for his mother.
Thus the heavy pack.
Then bus roared into view and David walked out the door toward it before Enrique could ask anything that might jeopardize his story.

He rests his hand on my knee as if I belong with him.
Blinding electricity shoots through me.

We get on the bus that will take us across the border.
In Nicaragua, no one is looking for me.
No one knows me.
No one in the entire country cares what I do.
No one has ever seen me before or will ever see me again.
No one knows Enrique or María or Martín.
The bus leaves Liberia and cruises north, up the smooth highway.
It feels like flying to freedom.
David and I sit close in our bus seat.
He kisses me on the mouth in broad daylight.
No one stares.
No one notices.
No one knows that I left my husband without saying goodbye and that this is another man.
I am not Diana, now.
Today, I am finally no one.

We make up a story for the family as the Guanacaste savannah rushes by outside the window.
David says we will say we've been together for five years.
I am his esposa.
In my country I would be called his girlfriend, but here, living with a man makes me his wife.
A pang of guilt knots my stomach.
Then it dissolves in the sweet taste of revenge for the humiliation of Enrique's women.
I look out the window and realize that nothing matters.
I am numb.
It doesn't matter to me that David is in love with me and that I am not in love with him.

It doesn't matter to me that Enrique is at home not eating.
It doesn't matter to me that I am lying to David's family, lying to Enrique's family, and lying to my own family.
It doesn't matter to me that I am wasting the money I need.
It doesn't matter to me that I should be grieving, but instead I am holding the hand of this beautiful boy whom I will also leave.
In a little over two weeks, I will be on a Delta Airlines flight into Atlanta and behind me there will be ashes and smoke and brokenness no matter what.

❦

Enrique bought me an ankle-length leopard print dress. I would never have chosen it for myself, but I had to admit, when I tried it on, it was beautiful on me—straight and simple with a deep side slit so that I didn't have to walk like a geisha. I was wearing it the night he forgot about me.

He really did forget about me. Completely.

It was Saturday. All day, I taught my classes at the University in Santa Cruz. Teaching made me feel like an intelligent human being, like I wasn't wasting my life no matter who might think I was. Students addressed me as "profesora," raised their hands, said please and thank you. No one insulted me or called me mean names. No one would have dreamed of it.

And then evening was falling and classes were over. I walked with my heavy bag of books to the street corner by the vegetable seller where I waited for Enrique to come in the car to take me home. I couldn't feel my feet after a day of standing, and I was very hungry. I hoped Enrique would be smiling when he pulled up, freshly bathed, dashing, with too much cologne and the music far too loud and want to take me to dinner. Sometimes he did that.

He didn't come.

I waited, and he didn't come.

I could have walked to the public phones on the other side of the plaza, but who would I call? There was one semi-public phone in Los Ríos and it was no use I call it. I didn't need all of Los Ríos to know that Enrique hadn't shown.

It got dark. Taxis stopped, asking if I needed a lift. I smiled sweetly and said, "No, gracias." Hours passed. I stood there fighting back tears. In my beautiful leopard print dress.

I had the money for a taxi. But if Enrique came for me and I wasn't waiting, there would be hell to pay. Hell. It was better to endure the lesser hell of waiting, the humiliation of being the woman in the beautiful dress on the street corner, forgotten. Unwanted.

Dinner time came and went.

Bedtime arrived. I became scared. Where was Enrique? He couldn't have forgotten me. If he didn't come for me, it meant something was wrong—either he couldn't come because something had happened to him or to the car or to both, or… Or the unthinkable. That he was drunk somewhere. That he had broken his sober streak and was someplace else with someone else, being an imbecile while his beautiful intelligent professor wife stood hungry and teary-eyed on a street corner, waiting. For four hours. I didn't feel beautiful or intelligent anymore. I felt horrible and stupid, like the worst, most pathetic kind of fool.

I gave up and took a taxi to Los Ríos. My heart pounded with dread the whole way. When I got home, my house was dark. There was no car in the driveway. The dog was hungry and needed water.

I showered, ate a piece of bread, and lay on my bed in the dark, too miserable to sleep. The unbearable night dragged on for eons. Eventually, dawn arrived. I wondered if I was a widow. I wondered if I would need a divorce. I wondered if Enrique would think of an excuse I could forgive him for. Part of me hoped he would.

I got up, fed the dog, watered the plants, and made coffee. It was 7:30 AM on Sunday morning when the car pulled into the driveway.

Part III: Nicaragua

David's family lives on the poor outskirts of Rivas.
We get off the bus and David leads me over broken streets to Tía Marta's house.
She is the widow of one of the murdered uncles.
David says Tía Marta has a big house with plenty of room for us to stay.
No one knows we are coming, and David is delighted by the surprise we will create.
They will be happy, he assures me.
They will love me.
He will introduce me to his step-father, José, he says, and José's new wife Alba.
They are more than blood family to him.
Tía Marta sees us walking up the street and the commotion begins.
She stands up from her rocking chair on the front porch, shouts, laughs, and calls something into the house.

A LUCKY BREATH

Cousins appear from all sides, running back and forth.
Dogs bark and jump.
Everyone hugs and kisses everyone.
Tía Marta cries because of how much David looks like her dead husband.
Neighbor ladies stare at us, eyeing me shyly with dubious smiles.
They ask me if I understand Spanish.

A man comes running up the dusty street followed by a young woman and two little girls.
He clasps David in a long hug, not letting him go.
This is José, the only father David has ever known.
José is the ex-husband of David's mother, the man who claimed David at birth, and raised him as his own son.
The woman arrives.
Her name is Alba, José's young wife.
The two wide-eyed little girls are their daughters, another set of sisters for David.
I can see that David belongs with them.
They argue with David that we must stay with them in their house down the street, but David knows they have only two beds.
He says we cannot do this.
They say we must.
They say the little girls can sleep with them in their bed.
David asks if the beds have mattresses.
They drop their gaze and say they do not.
David says we will stay with Tía Marta tonight, and tomorrow we will buy mattresses.
Then we will sleep in their house.
They say alright.

Tía Marta owns a brick house in a neighborhood where the other homes are made of wood and tin.

She has a cement floor instead of pressed dirt, and she has some indoor plumbing on a street with one other communal faucet.

Tía Marta is considered rich because from the front room of her home she operates a small grocery store.

She and her daughter sell things like canned tuna, rice, milk, toilet paper, laundry soap, light bulbs, sugar, and coffee to the neighbors.

This house has two bedrooms, a living room with a vinyl couch, a bathroom, and a wooden lean-to kitchen through the back door.

In the bathroom, there is a seatless toilet in one corner, a crooked dripping sink in another, and in a third, a pipe points from the wall near the ceiling.

The water that pours from the pipe onto the floor and down the drain by the wall is our shower.

In the entrance to the bathroom, a shower curtain is the only door.

At night, after we have eaten our plates of rice and beans, Tía Marta gives her daughter's room to David and me for the night. The girl will sleep with her.

Even at this hottest time of year, we must pull the wooden windows closed against thieves at night, filling the room with a stifling blackness thick as cream.

A purring pedestal fan in the corner slightly stirs the soup of hot air.

This is our first night together.

We find each other in the dark.

The tiny bed protests our every move.

Interior walls in homes are partitions that don't reach to roofs,

and we can hear Tía Marta's sleepy breathing.
Giggling, we vacate the impossibly noisy bed.
I lie with David on the bare cement floor, blindly, mutely making love in the suffocating dark.
I think of the cockroaches that must be sliding up and down the walls.
I think of scorpions I cannot see.
I think of my husband.
I think of my husband with his other women.
I refuse to think about my husband.
The April heat and the lover I can finally have after so much waiting do not let me rest.
Dawn is near when we fall asleep.

My parents came to visit Enrique and me in our new house. I cleaned furiously, trying to make everything as perfect as possible for their arrival. We drove to San José to pick them up at the airport in the car they'd given us, spent the night crammed into Lenny's house with his wife and daughters, then came home the next day. I translated for everyone until my tongue tired and I couldn't remember which language was which.

Once before, when I lived with Mateo and Norma, my parents visited Los Ríos. On that visit, Mateo and Norma gave my parents and I their double bed because it was the best they had to offer, and Mateo and Norma slept in the single bed that was normally mine. This time my parents had their own bed in their own bedroom. We giggled about how, on their first visit, nobody got any sleep.

My mother brought me the beautiful white curtains she made for our windows. We cleaned the house together and hung the new curtains in place of the sheets I'd draped over the rods. My father played his guitar on the porch after dinner the way he did on summer evenings on the home farm. Adán and Miguel came over and, unaware that Amazing Grace is a religious song, danced silly jigs that sent my parents into mortified hysterics. They'd never met someone who didn't recognize the melody of Amazing Grace.

On Saturday I took them to the University with me where they watched me teach my drama and literature classes. Enrique came home after he finished working at the pottery workshop, ate dinner with us, and sat on the couch watching a movie on TV. On Sunday, instead of going to church as we would have at home, my mother cleaned the house with me and hung the clothes on the line in the back yard as I washed them. Then we dressed in our best outfits and went to a fiesta to watch drunk men ride angry bulls. We ate ice cream cones and skewers of roasted meat. Enrique drank Coca-Cola and held my hand.

They only stayed for a week. The farm in Pennsylvania needed its farmers, so their visits were always short. All week, Enrique was an angel. He was as timid in the presence of my parents as he had once been in mine. When he first started coming over to Mateo and Norma's house to work on pottery with Mateo, Enrique wouldn't eat if I was in the room. He could hardly look at me. While my parents were our guests, he did thoughtful things like refill the water pitcher in the refrigerator and sweep the dusty front porch. He came home every evening, and stayed. He didn't stomp, snort, slam doors, hurl insults, or disappear. He smiled shyly and turned on the TV so quietly only he could hear it. My parents loved him. Their initial disapproval of our marriage melted away. Enrique could be as endearing as a puppy any day he decided to.

I loved Enrique for not embarrassing me. I loved him because I loved him. All I needed was for him to let me.

The image of our marriage that my parents took home, although it was mostly false, was the image of the marriage I wanted. The marriage I thought I was getting when I signed the paper on that hot day in Santa Cruz. The marriage I believed was entirely possible if I could just get my half of it right.

David takes me to José and Alba's house.
They welcome us home as if we will never leave.
Alba, my new suegra, is ten years younger than I am.
José, my new suegro, is ten years older.
The house is built of weathered slabs of wood and has a dirt floor.
One bedroom is divided into two by a curtain on a rope.
On one side of the curtain there is a double bed where the four of them will sleep.
On the other side is a single bed for David and me.
There is no running water.
In the kitchen stands a woodstove made of mud, a cement sink where dishes are washed with water from a yellow bucket, and a table for preparing food.
In the living room, a wooden bench stands by the wall.
There is a small TV, a table, and two chairs.
Leaves blow in through the spaces between the weather-warped boards that form the walls.
Because we are guests, David and I are seated at the table on the two chairs to eat our meals.
We drink from the two water glasses, and receive the family's two spoons when Alba serves us plates of food.
The little girls eye me mutely.
When I smile at them, they turn to each other, unsure of what to do.
David teases them in the gentle charming way he knows from raising his other little sisters.
They giggle.
Soon they are sitting on his knees curiously examining his one

ear ring and the delicate wooden cross he wears tied around his neck.

Each city block in this outer area of Rivas has a public tap with potable water.
Each family owns several buckets which they fill and carry home for bathing, cooking, cleaning, and washing clothes.
Luckily for us, the water faucet is next door, so we don't have to carry our buckets as far as most.
A man named Manduko lives next door to us.
This is lucky for us because Manduko loves to do helpful tasks.
He is a young adult with Down's Syndrome.
At first, I am afraid of him.
He is wildly uninhibited, and I can't understand a word he says.
He shouts at me as if I were deaf when I don't understand him.
I stare helplessly at David, who laughs.
Manduko carries water for us.
He carries water for everyone.
For this reason, he is never hungry, and he lives in a neighborhood of friends.
Manduko brings buckets of water for Alba to wash the dishes, and buckets of water for washing our clothes.
He brings buckets of water for our baths.
Manduko loves David.
David teases him like a brother, and Manduko laughs his joyful laugh.
As the days pass, I begin to decipher his sounds and he stops shouting at me in frustration.

The bath is behind the house near the pila for hand-washing clothes.

It is a squarish enclosure formed by four poles planted in the ground, walled by shoulder-high tin and cloth.
There is a board to stand on, to keep your feet from getting muddy while you use a small plastic dish to scoop water over yourself from the bucket Manduko carried.
You can look over the tin and chat with the neighbors while you wash your hair.
You can yell at the dog to leave the chickens alone.
In the back of each lot, each home has an outhouse.
Adults use the outhouses, but children are not expected to.
Small children, who rarely wear a full set of clothes and often none at all, squat in the dirt.

When I wash David's and my clothes in the pila under the mango tree, the little girls on the block come to stare at me.
No one tells them staring is rude.
To them, it is not rude.
They have never seen a foreign woman wash clothes.
They expect I will need help.
They ask me, "Sabe usted lavar?"
I answer them, "Sí," hoping they will go away, but still they stand watching in amazement.
They run to tell their mothers, then return to stare again.
Soon, the mothers are peering shyly from their windows at me as I sweat.
I try not to waste the water Manduko carries for me, bucket after bucket.
Washing clothes by hand in a pila is nothing new for me.
In Los Ríos I left behind a small semi-automatic washing machine, but before I owned it, I scrubbed our clothes by hand the way clothes have been washed since the dawn of time.
I scoop water over each piece, sprinkle powdered soap, then scrub with a hard-earned deftness, rolling and unrolling shirts

and shorts against the rough cement surface of the pila.
I beat them up and down, attack stains with a special bush, then pour more of the precious water Manduko kindly carries. Then wring hard with my strong wrists and arms, hang the pieces on the line in the sun, and begin again.

Alba smiles at me.

David is proud.

I think about washing Enrique's clothes in the pila in Santa Cruz back when he loved me.

I wish I was in Santa Cruz with Enrique when he loved me, not in Rivas pretending to be David's wife.

Not with a plane ticket to Atlanta and no idea what to do when I land.

I decide to forget it.

I smile at David and blow him a kiss.

The little neighbor girls laugh.

In the rainy season, two years after we scandalized Los Ríos by moving into that furnitureless little rental house in Santa Cruz, Enrique and I moved into our very own home in Los Ríos. Strangely, I vaguely remember the day we moved in. Surely someone lent us a truck which we must have loaded with our couch, the kitchen table and chairs, and the bed. We put our clothes in green garbage bags and knotted them shut.

It was a beautiful little house, imperfect in the ways that houses in Guanacaste are imperfect, and perfect in the ways that they are right. The faucet in the bathroom sink dripped from the first day it was installed, and the lights were just light bulbs in sockets on beams, but it was made especially for me. The wash sink on the back porch was the tallest one in town, exactly the way I needed it to be. The tiled breakfast bar and oversized front windows were luxury items that delighted me. Lenny built me shelves under the kitchen counter and enclosed them with glass doors. Enrique bought a plexiglass sliding door for the shower, a feature so fancy I couldn't believe it belonged to me. In the daytime, I tied back the long white curtains that my mother made me. At night, they hung loose, shifting like spirits in the night breeze.

It was a bright, clean house compared to the others we'd lived in. I put our clothes in the wardrobe, made the bed, and chose places in the kitchen for the dishes, the silverware, and the pots and pans. I set our soap and shampoo in the shower. It was a simple move; we didn't have a lot of things. I hung pretty sheets up at the windows while I waited for my parents to visit and bring me the curtains. The extra bedroom became my own precious space, with my desk by the window, and my books.

I thought the house looked lonely in the grass with no trees or flowers around it. I told Enrique I wanted to buy plants. He agreed to the idea, but every afternoon I suggested we go to the vivero, he said he didn't have time. The rainy season was ending, and soon the chance to plant anything that would survive the dry season would be over until next year. I went by myself.

Twice, I went to Santa Cruz, filled our little car with greenery, and drove home peering through the foliage. I bought a coconut palm, ornamental palms, lilies, cacti, flowering trees, and pretty-colored flowers that I forgot the names of. I borrowed a digging iron and a shovel from Martín and started making holes. Martín watched me work, amused and somewhat embarrassed that I was doing it all myself. Angel offered to help. Enrique smiled and shook his head at the blisters on my hands. The old woman who lives on the other side of the road gave me cuttings from everything she had that would grow if you poke a piece of it into the ground, and I kept on planting.

I spent windy summer sunsets circling the house with the hose, pondering every plant, inspecting each one for signs of growth. The roble, the malinche and the cortes amarillo become large trees, so I planted them farther away, out of the reach of my garden hose. I filled buckets of water that I carried to them. Enrique shook his head. He said I was crazy. He growled that robles are bad trees because they attract lightning strikes. I smiled, wondering why, if they attract lightning, are there so many of them?

Something in the back of my mind whispered to me that I would never trim the bushes or sit in the shade of these trees. As I dug the holes and placed the palms, as I carried water to the malinche and coaxed the hibiscus to keep on trying, I knew. I didn't want to believe it. I refused to think about it. I loved Los Ríos, Enrique, and this house. But the melody was losing its tune.

When Enrique was home, he watched TV at inconceivable decibels, and he didn't want to be interrupted. If I turned it down, he turned it louder. But mostly, he just wasn't there. Where was Enrique? I rarely had any idea. He roared away in the car when I brought it home from work, leaving only dust clouds and evenings of silence. The house was a beautiful empty shell.

I pushed it out of my mind like a bad dream. Everything would be fine. Any day now.

I spend my money.
I don't want to spend my money.
I can't spend my money.
The money from the truck is all I have.
It has to take me to Atlanta.
It has to feed me and house me while I find a job.
It has to buy me a wardrobe of work clothes in Atlanta—everything from underwear to an overcoat.
Decent shoes.
It has to finance my graduate school applications.
I have nothing else.

But David knows I sold the truck for a million colones.
When he promises his family simple foam mattresses for their beds, I agree.
This is something they need.
And how else will I sleep?
I am happy to do this.
I don't realize what is beginning.
José's blue car from the 1970's sits immobile in the yard, awaiting a minor repair.
David suggests we fix it for him since for two weeks we will live in his house.
I would not think of saying no.
But the repairs to the car never end.
Each time the mechanic replaces something and starts the engine, the next link in the chain fails.
For every kilometer the car travels, it needs something new to make the next one.
For two weeks, I buy part after part, always one repair away

from a perfect car.
I have money, and I must share it openhandedly.
This is the unwritten law of family, here.
I know this.
What is mine is David's.
What is David's is his family's.
They have given us everything they have: their beds and their spoons.
We have told them I am his wife.

The family needs food.
We buy food.
Food is cheap in Nicaragua, and we feed the family: rice, beans, coffee, eggs, cabbage, tuna, pork, and milk for the little girls.
We buy a set of tin silverware with plastic handles.

Now everyone will eat with a spoon when meals are served.

※

I'd just arrived home from an afternoon of varnishing window and door frames at our new house when the thunderstorm unleashed. The black clouds overhead split open and suddenly the amount of water moving from the sky to the earth was like a river flowing down on the world. The press of it seemed to flatten the trees and the sound on the tin roof that kept me dry was deafening. Outside the windows and doors, the grey wall of vertical water breathed its cool breath.

I took off my clothes and stepped into the shower but when I turned the handle, nothing happened. This didn't worry me—interruptions in the water and electricity service were common in Costa Rica. But I was so sweaty and dirty after my afternoon of work that the idea of no shower was unbearable.

I took the soap, the shampoo, and my towel and walked naked out the back door of the little wooden house. Under the giant gushing sky, each dip in the corrugated tin roof formed a spout of fresh clean water that shot into the air and down onto the grass. I caught my breath when the spouts of cool water hit my steaming shoulders, tilted my head back and let the rain bath wash through my grimy hair.

Enrique wasn't home, or he would have thrown a fit. I hoped Enrique wouldn't show up and catch me. But no one lived behind the house, and the field that stretched off into the distance was filled with nothing but torrential rain. Thunder shook the ground and lightening sizzled through the air. I shampooed my hair in the rain shower, soaped my body, and rinsed away all the suds and the dirt. The storm thundered on.

When Enrique pulled the car up to the house later and dashed inside through the downpour, I was dressed and calmly sipping rainwater coffee while I prepared English reading comprehension exercises for my university students, freshly ionized and perfumed.

A LUCKY BREATH

At the city market, David wants boots.
He asks me to buy them for him.
He tries them on and struts.
"Qué piensa?" he asks.
"Mira que buenas."
They are beautiful boots, and strong.
His one pair of collapsing sneakers stares back at me.
I don't know what to say.
When will it stop?
I don't know what to do.
I buy them for him so he will stop pleading.
I buy him boots that cost more than food for a week.
He wears them proudly around town, but I am not proud.
I am confused and somehow ashamed.
In David's mind, we are rich.
In my mind, I am poor and getting poorer.
We take the family to the beach for a day, because by now everyone has heard that David and his wife have money.
My other choice is to run away again, and I can't.
I don't have the strength.
We take a trip to Masaya, accompanied by David's cousins.
They all say I must see Masaya.
The tourist market is full of beautiful things for sale.
I numbly bleed money as if from a wound too deep to hurt.
I watch it flow out of me and experience fear, but no pain.

We spend hot afternoons in the shade of the back yard with David's Maná tapes playing in José's old boom-box.
One of the neighbor girls muses about how she would cut her hair if she had the money.

"Yo se lo puedo cortar," I offer.
This is something I can give that costs me nothing.
Her eyes widen and shine.
She does not doubt me.
She has watched me wash.
Somebody produces a dull scissors, and David gets a towel.
As her long tangled hair falls at my feet, other neighbor women and girls gather around to watch.
"¿Cuánto cuesta?" they ask.
"Nada," I say.
All afternoon, I cut hair in the hot Nicaraguan shade.
I cut the hair of shy neighbor women who can barely look at me, and of jubilant little girls.
I slice away the shaggy locks of little boys who sit frozen in terrified delight.
The neighbors gossip and laugh, pretending this is a real beauty shop, feeling beautiful in their newly-cropped hair.
My scissors snip until the sun has sunken and my hand is aching.
It costs me nothing but love and time.
I have enough of both.
It is the best gift I give in Rivas, better than the car parts, mattresses, or spoons.

A LUCKY BREATH

On Saturdays, I was an English professor. I've never had a job I loved as much as I loved teaching literature classes in English at the Universidad Latina in Santa Cruz. In those days, the University held its classes on the high school campus on Saturdays. I was handed a sheet of objectives to meet each semester, but the miniscule University library had no books in English around which I could construct my courses. I called my parents and asked them to mail me some of my own books as quickly as possible, and in the meantime, I borrowed books and stories from the shelves of American friends in Playa Celeste.

In the first class, we read Charlotte's Web. I made up vocabulary lists, worksheets, group exercises, and creative writing assignments for adult students whose education had prepared them only to memorize and repeat. When I asked my students what they thought about what they read, they didn't understand the question. They thought I was crazy.

I persisted, made them laugh, began to drag their own ideas out of them. Eventually, they caught on. They loved my classes, and so did I.

On Saturdays, I was smart. Everyone respected me. My students craved my approval. No one would have dared to call me idiota, estupida, perezosa. No one would have wanted to. People raised their hands and waited to ask me questions. They said "please", "thank you", and "may I ask you a question?" Nobody shouted at me on Saturdays. No one ignored me. Anyone who was late apologized. When I asked something, hands shot up. No one shouted or stormed out of the room because they didn't want to answer questions.

On Sundays, I worked. I cleaned the house and washed the clothes. Those things were my job even if I had to do them on Sun-

day. If I wanted to go with Enrique to watch soccer games or bull riding or to do anything fun with him, I had to finish my week's worth of domestic work on Sunday morning. By early afternoon, Enrique was in the car pulling out of the driveway. If I didn't want to be stuck sitting alone in an empty house doing nothing, I had to be finished and ready.

On Monday through Friday, I got up early and drove the car to Playa Celeste to teach Spanish to other foreigners at the shady stand where I sat displaying Enrique's pottery to passersby. In the late afternoon, I put away the pottery and hurried home, thinking about what to make for dinner, hoping I would find Enrique in a good mood. Hoping I would find Enrique, because you never knew. More often than not, I hurried home to prepare a meal that got cold while I waited hungrily. He would charge into the house gruffly, after dark, scolding me about anything so that I would not ask where he had been. Sometimes I asked anyway even though he would glare at me in reply and either not answer or say something ridiculous. But not always. Once in a while he was the sweet and gentle man I'd fallen in love with. Just often enough for me to hope it really was my fault and that I could make it better by trying harder.

But Saturdays were my day. On Saturday, I was beautiful in my dress and pretty sandals, hair pulled back, a book in one hand and chalk in the other. When I gave instructions, everyone followed them. When I said, "Great work, see you next week," they stared at me disappointedly. No one wanted to leave. Neither did I.

There is a place here in Nicaragua where I want to go.
I want to cross the lake to the island of the volcanoes.
From the waters of Lake Nicaragua, two enormous volcanoes rise into the sky, forming the island of Ometepe.
One is called Concepción; one is called Maderas.
Volcan Concepción, the tall one, billows steam into the sky.
Sleepy Volcan Maderas holds a reservoir of water in its crater.
A dilapidated ferry chugs back and forth across the dark water from the mainland to the fertile island shores several times each day.
The towering fire volcano speaks to me.
It beckons me.
I want to cross the dark water on the little boat.
I want to press my hands and feet to its soil, to sleep in its shadow and to feel its presence blocking the stars.
To witness a living volcano is to witness the beginning and the end—the creation of the world and its destruction, in one single event.
I too am being created and destroyed at this very moment.
The fire mountain calls me.

I tell David I want to go to Ometepe.
We pack a bag and board the creaking wooden ferry to the island.
The boat is blue, or used to be.
The seats we sit on have been removed from a yellow school bus like the one I rode to Mastersonville Elementary School in 1977.
Muscular brown men load the hold with bulk quantities of rice, beans, cans of tuna, vegetable oil, soda crackers, cornmeal,

dog food, and toilet paper.
The tireless boat churns through the water carrying families, individuals, island people with business on the mainland, mainland people with business on the island.
The towering cone of active Concepción grows taller and taller as we approach until it has taken over the earth and sky.

When David and I step off the boat onto the island, we don't know what to do next.
We have never been across the water.
There is lodging in the small port town where the ferry empties, refills, and turns around, but it is only mid-afternoon.
I don't want to rent a room now.
David will want to go inside and close the door.
I want to explore this place.

A friendly stranger suggests we go to Santo Domingo on the other side of the island.
He says it's beautiful and that you can see both volcanoes from Santo Domingo.
He offers to drive us in his car for what we all know is a ridiculous amount of money.
When we say no, he points us to a bus that is turning onto the street, leaving for Santo Domingo now.
This is a quintessential third world bus, crammed to the roof with no limits and no rules, people and their possessions bursting from the doors and windows.
In Costa Rica, buses are not like this one.
In Costa Rica, there are rules.
In Costa Rica, there are more buses.
I can't imagine how a bus is transported from the mainland of Nicaragua to the island of Ometepe.
It would sink the blue wooden ferry.

Perhaps that's why there are so few.
We can get on this one somehow, or we can wait until tomorrow.
We crush our bodies into the infernally hot bus where there is no room for us.

We don't know it, but we have begun a three-hour pilgrimage.
The bus has the atmosphere of a family reunion—noisy, jubilant, and we are the only strangers.
Because we are guests, and because I am clearly a foreigner, we are allowed to sit beside the driver on the hump that houses the engine.
There is no pavement on Ometepe.
We bump and jostle over rocks and ruts through the dust as the sun slides slowly down the sky.
The mountain cone, stately as God, never disappears from our left.
A deep peace soothes me on the terrible bus.
I am thirsty and hot, very uncomfortable, pressed on all sides by the sweat of strangers.
I am on a bus lost in the foothills of an island in an unfamiliar country.
I am invisible.
My mother doesn't know where I am.
My husband doesn't know where I am.
My friends don't know where I am.
Only David knows where I am, and he is invisible, too.
Everything stops hurting.
I feel I have stopped existing or thinking, stopped suffering.
Like I have died, kind of, and find myself in this silent place on this noisy bus on this beautiful island so close to God.
I stare out the window of the bus at the landscape of Ometepe.
An ox walks down the road toward us with his deliberate plodding steps.

A woman rides on his back.
We approach each other, the plodding beast and the rattling bus.
The woman loosely holds a rope which passes through a ring in the ox's nose.
I see that she is a young woman—a girl, really.
In her arms she is holding a bundle.
As we pass her on the dusty road, I see through the window that the bundle is a tiny infant.
What is her name?
Where is she going?
Who is waiting for her there?
What does she fear?
Whom does she love?

The girl-woman is no one.
Her baby is no one.
I am no one.
David is no one.
And here we are together on this road, slowly passing in opposite directions.
I am so far from home.
I have no home.
I am nowhere.
A white face on a yellow bus between brown hills under a blue sky.
I want nothing.
I am nothing.
The bus lumbers on.
I evaporate into peace.

David and I arrive in Santo Domingo at sunset.
We find a small hospedaje where we are the only guests.

A LUCKY BREATH

After the owner cooks us dinner, we walk to the shore of the lake.
We abandon our clothes in a pile on the sand and go night-swimming in the warm blackness of Lake Nicaragua on the far side of Ometepe.
The cone of Concepción watches over us against the stars.
We make love in the lake where freshwater sharks lurk.

Enrique said we should get a dog. The construction crew was working on our house every day, and soon we would move in. All houses in Los Ríos have dogs, chickens, and sometimes a pig to fatten for Christmas or Easter. He said we should get chickens. The pup we would want and the chickens we would raise needed to grow up before they would be any use, so it was time to get started. Enrique came home with a little black puppy that appeared to be part rottweiler, and said his name was going to be Coqui.

Coqui was silly, naughty, smart, and wanted to please us. His only weakness was the little chicks Enrique brought from María's house. We were supposed to be starting a flock that would provide us with eggs and meat for years to come, but Coqui couldn't leave them alone. He was too young and sweet to have killing in mind, but the chicks he played with never survived the games.

On a rare Saturday when there were no classes at the university, I took him with me when I went to admire the progress on the new house. I rode up the street on my bike with Coqui trotting along beside me. Everything distracted him, but when I called to him, he followed. Enrique was at the site helping the workers. They needed something, he said. A package of screws, a bag of mortar, a tube of silicon—I don't remember. Enrique asked if I would go to Santa Cecilia two kilometers down the road and get it at the little hardware store. I said yes, but the car was parked at our house and it was going to take me some time on my bicycle. One of the neighbors suggested I drive his motorcycle. I'd driven a motorcycle a few times and I was confident I could teeter two kilometers down a country road and back with the small item they needed.

I took off on the motorcycle. Coqui followed me. I stopped and called to Enrique to come get him. Enrique waved me on and said just to go slowly and make sure he didn't get lost. Slowly was the only way I knew how to go. I should have done anything but let that silly pup follow me down the road.

I should have gone home and locked him in the house even if he peed on the floor or chewed the couch. But we were both inexperienced and we were both having fun.

I drove carefully and Coqui bounded behind me to the hardware store. I made my purchase, and turned the motorcycle toward Los Ríos. On the way back, a neighbor woman in a small rickety pick-up truck passed us and I didn't see what happened. I heard the thump, Coqui's screams, the truck breaking.

He wasn't dead, but he couldn't stand up. We put my wailing pup in the back of the pickup truck and she drove him back home. I drove home too, trying not to cry. Enrique was going to kill me. This was going to be all my fault. He told me to go, and told me to let Coqui follow me, but it was still going to be my fault. There would be something that I would have done wrong, even though Enrique hadn't been present to see what it was, and it was going to be my fault that our dog was hit by the pick-up. I tried to stop hearing the awful canine scream, but I couldn't.

There was a lot of commotion when I got back to Los Ríos. Enrique was already at the house making Coqui a bed. I was lucky that day—Enrique blamed the driver of the truck for Coqui's injury, not me. With Enrique, every day was a game of Russian Roulette. That day I got off scot-free.

Coqui never got up again. He ate a little, drank a little, and dirtied the spot where he lay. Enrique took him to the vet and the vet said his back had broken and we'd have to put him down. Coqui looked sweetly at us, wagged his tail a little, and laid his head on his paws. Rather than pay the vet for an injection, Enrique brought him home and called Mateo to come over with his shotgun.

I never saw Enrique so undone as he was when Mateo came into the yard carrying that gun. He walked wordlessly into the *house and closed the door. In the farthest corner of the house was the bathroom. Enrique walked into the bathroom. I followed him. He went into the shower. I followed him there too. He cringed in the corner of the shower with his hands over his ears and his forehead against the wall. I buried my face in his back and hugged him as we waited for the shot.*

A LUCKY BREATH

※

In the morning, we leave Ometepe and return to the mainland.

David suggests we go to Managua, the capital.
Uncle Roberto, the spared younger brother, lives there with his wife.
Roberto had a job as an accountant for a hospital until it ran out of money and stopped paying him.
Now, he is hoping for a new job.
Roberto's wife sells shoes in the shoe aisle of the grocery store.
We can stay with them, David says.
I think, why not?
Managua, now or never.

Managua is hot.
Costa Rica's capital sets in a highland valley.
Managua is in a sweltering and humid lowland.
Beside the city lies a murdered lake, dead white and breathless.
Roberto meets us at the bus station, hugs us, and cries because of how much David looks like his father.
David cries too.
Roberto has a car because he used to have money, so we get in the car.
We drive through the heart of Managua.
It is a spider web of streets with no discernable order.
I ask where the city center is.
They say this is the city center.
Roberto takes us to the new mall.
He thinks I will like it because I am American.
It will hurt his feelings if I tell him I don't care about American malls, so I exclaim about how beautiful it is.
It is shiny and artificial-looking.

We order Chinese food in a food court.
Roberto and David frown suspiciously at the mushrooms in their rice.
Neither of them has ever eaten this thing before.
They find the mushrooms amusing and less offensive than they expected.

They explain to me about the war, the bombings, how the good guys beat the bad guys but then somehow weren't so good anymore.
I try to follow along.
They tell me about the earthquake that came before the war began, but always factors in as part of the war story, as if the earth itself took sides.
It's confusing.

We get in the car again to continue sight-seeing.
I expect to observe ruins everywhere, but the ruins are gone.
Managua, instead, is a construction zone.
The war ended ten years before, and now the city is being rebuilt.
Everyone hopes that one day it will be beautiful.
There are sculptures and statues, parks, paintings, and monuments throughout the city, in various stages of completion.
The streets here are better constructed and maintained than the ones in Costa Rica.
Drivers are even more lawless.

Roberto says he was ten when his older brothers were shot.
He says soldiers rounded up young men from the streets and shot them or dropped them into the ocean from airplanes to keep them from joining the enemy.
If you were out in the streets after dark, you probably wouldn't make it home.

A LUCKY BREATH

I ask who the good guys were at that time, and no one seems to understand the question.
I try asking who the bad guys were.
Still, the question cannot be answered.
No one in the story, except the murdered boys, is truly good.

Enrique wanted to build a house, and he talked about it constantly. People don't rent houses in Los Ríos; they live in the house they're born in until they build their own. If they are never able, they just stay, adding layer after layer to the family. We, on the other hand, had just moved for the second time in six months. The old wooden house where we first lived beside Mateo and Norma turned out not to be as great of a deal as we thought. The owner got cold feet about having occupants, worried we might get so comfortable we wouldn't want to leave, and she anticipated the remodel. We'd barely gotten settled when we had to pack up again.

It was ok. We found another house. This one had the same lovely wooden windows to push open to the sunshine every morning, but it also had indoor plumbing. No more visits to the outhouse or chamber pots at night. It wasn't free, however. And again, it was someone else's house; someday they were going to want it back. This thought tormented Enrique. His brothers and our friends shook their heads with pity for us, imagining the day we would have nowhere to live again.

Martín, who always intended one day to divide his property between his five sons, contacted a topographer and a lawyer.

We didn't have money to build, nor did we have anything to offer the bank in exchange for a loan. I told my parents that Martín had given Enrique land for us to put a house on. I asked if they would lend us money to build a simple home. When my parents learned how little it would cost to construct a cement house with a tin roof like all the others in Los Ríos and in the province, they said we wouldn't need to pay them back.

In the evenings, we sat with a pen drawing pictures in my notebook of what we wanted our house to look like. I wanted lots of large windows. Enrique shook his head and said that windows were expensive. I said I didn't mind. I wanted a bright breezy house that the sun would illuminate all day. I also asked for a deep shady porch for afternoon and evening lounging. Enrique thought a porch that large was a waste of money too and said it would always be dusty. He was right about the dust, but I insisted. I could picture us sitting there swatting mosquitoes and lazily chatting as night fell.

When we went to pick the floor tiles, I chose marbled blue because to me they felt cool like water. Our little two-bedroom house sprouted and grew like a plant in the meadow beside the house where Enrique was born.

In my free hours, I sanded and varnished the window and door frames before the glass came, while the air shifted through. Enrique helped the building crew by running errands to Santa Cruz for more grout, kitchen and bathroom faucets, and to order glass for the windows. Martín spent morning and evening hours spraying water from a hose onto the fresh cement so that it would dry slowly, preventing the sun from crumbling our house as fast as the men constructed it.

I loved that I would have my own house in Los Ríos. I'd always known I belonged here. And maybe, when we had our own house, Enrique would be happy like he used to be. He would be proud of it and love it and want to be there with me.

Roberto wants to show me a monument.
I think it will be a pillar or a statue, but it isn't.
The monument is a stone cube in the grass.
Roberto says that under it is a pit where the Sandinistas threw live dissenters and poured cement on them.
But wait, weren't the Sandinistas the dissenters?
Sort of.
In the beginning they were.
The four sides of the monument that marks the place of this atrocity bear symbols.
One side has a Nicaraguan flag.
On another, a butterfly beside a bomb juxtapose vulnerability with willful destruction.
On another side, the figure of a man reminds of what lies below.
And lastly, a dove, bearing hope for peace.
I am moved by the symbolism being employed in this city's rebirth.

A woman stands watering the grass in the park.
Roberto and David reminisce with her about war times.
Everyone was hungry, they remember.
A pocket full of money bought you nothing, because there was nothing to buy.
Government commissaries stocked everything, and provisions were rationed according to the card you carried saying how many people were in your family.
I know nothing of rations or war.
All of my tragedies have been personal.

Next, Roberto takes us to Parque de La Paz.

A LUCKY BREATH

It is the site of another pit dug in the ground.
I observe the theme of remembering a buried history.
He tells the story of post-war president Violeta de Chamorro ordering the war weapons be deposited in the pit, then filling the pit with cement saying, "No longer will we bury our children because of arms, we will bury arms because of our children."
Guns drowned in cement cannot injure.
Roberto wipes his eyes when he says it.
He is thinking of his mother when they collected the bodies of the brothers.
One side of the pit has been excavated, revealing a crude wall with gun barrels and parts of tanks sticking out of the cement, frozen in their destructive purpose.
Tufts of grass grow on them.
In the center of the park, a tank stands doused in cement, rendered forever useless, a palm growing out of its center.
Cement has been used to silence so much.
Tears streak David's cheeks.
I brush them away and hug him.
I don't understand the war, but I understand pain.
Something of my innocence dies on this day.

 Enrique took Adán, Miguel, and me to Santa Cruz to see the Independence Day celebration.
 Central America celebrates its independence from Spain with a torch that is carried on foot from the north to the south, symbolizing the path the news of freedom traveled when it arrived. In Costa Rica, at each road that branches off from the main highway, runners wait to light torches from the fire of the mother torch. The torchbearers are elementary and high school students selected for this privilege by academic merit. They will run with this flame in their hands to their hometowns. Around mid-day, on the eve of Independence, the torch at Costa Rica's border takes fire from the Nicaraguan torch arriving from the north. A procession that will accompany the runners on their journey for the next 24 hours begins. The flame reaches Liberia and then branches southwest before it arrives in Santa Cruz well after midnight.

 At what would usually have been bedtime, we piled the boys in the car and took off. We stopped in other small villages, listened to live bands playing at community dances, ate ice cream, and drank Coca-Cola, doing everything we could think of to stay awake until midnight. Then we joined a long line of cars driving from the countryside surrounding Los Ríos into Santa Cruz to witness the arrival of the torch.
 I was sleepy. The boys were giddy. Enrique was in a good mood. I could barely believe that, as Enrique explained, that this was a school activity the boys would earn credit for attending, and that other families would be there, sober, in patriotic attendance in the middle of the night. The only other time I'd been in Santa Cruz in the middle of the night I was drunk at the fiesta and getting into trouble with Enrique.

We parked the car in front of the Banco Nacional on the main street in Santa Cruz and waited. A dizzying cacophony of music rose from all the waiting cars. The mood was exuberant. Some of the sleepiness in my head lifted.

Soon, car horns sounded in the distance, coming from the direction of Liberia. The marching band of high school students struck up a joyful ruckus. Enrique shouted at the boys to stop chasing each other around and over the car through the sunroof and to pay attention. The torch is received with reverence.

As runners with the burning torch arrived in Santa Cruz, runners from neighboring towns jogged alongside, reaching their dark torches into the fire and light, igniting symbols of freedom in the humid midnight. They then turned to run with this precious flame toward their homes, their beautiful faces bathed in the magic of the hour and freedom's fire. Over the music of the disastrous band sounded the slap of so many young feet on pavement, and the hiss—I hadn't imagined the hiss—of the fire leaping into the night, lighting the sweaty delighted faces. I hadn't imagined I would be moved nearly to tears, but I was. The freedom of the country was our freedom, granted, not taken in a war—a blessing to be received with gratitude and joy.

Students in the final grades of the school in Los Ríos were there. Friends and family cheered as these familiar children ignited the fire they would carry step by step on foot to our tiny town sleeping between the mountains. From Santa Cruz to Los Ríos, in a long procession of runners, horseback riders and drivers of cars and motorcycles, we accompanied the good news over hills and through valleys to our very own plaza. It was after 3 AM when we arrived. Adán and Miguel slept in a jumble on the back seat.

Enrique roused them when we arrived at the public hall by the plaza in Los Ríos. Inside the hall, their teacher, the school director, and all the families we normally saw during the day, were wide *awake and chatting, waiting for the procession with the burning torch.*

A ceremony followed, but I didn't see it. My eyes were too heavy with all that I'd seen that night. Enrique shook his head at me and chided me for missing the tamales and hot coffee at dawn after a school presentation. But the clock showed an inconceivable hour to endure a school presentation sitting on a backless wooden stool, so I chose my pillow instead.

A LUCKY BREATH

✣

At night back in Rivas David and I lie whispering on our little bed.
The moon and the streetlight shine into the bedroom between the boards that form the walls.
Wind blows through the house.
Something runs across my feet.
I squeal, shiver, and leap into a sitting position.
I tell David a mouse ran across the bed, and he laughs.
I make him turn on the light because I want to be sure it's gone.
It isn't gone.
It isn't a mouse.
It is a cockroach bigger than the biggest cockroach I have ever imagined.
It is almost as big as my hand and it is on my bed.
My panic causes fits of muffled hysteria among the rest of the family.
David says "Mira," and I see more.
They are everywhere.
There is one on the ceiling.
More on the wall.
I ask what is happening.
I haven't seen these monsters before, ever, on any other night.
I think I am tough about bugs, but this is a horror movie.
David says they are mating at the full moon.
He says to lie down, that they won't hurt me.
I know they won't hurt me.
But they are horrible and I hate them.
What if they walk on me?
What if I wake up with one on my face or inside my clothes?

I have no choice but to get back into bed.
I wrap the sheet around me tightly on all sides and curl up as small as I can, breathing through a tiny hole.
I tell David that tomorrow I am going to buy all the roach spray in Rivas.
I don't care what it costs.
He giggles himself to sleep and snores lightly.
I lie in a miserably hot knot praying for mercy.

We visit David's only tía.
This tía is the sister who lost her brothers to bullets against a wall.
She runs an unofficial neighborhood bar from her kitchen.
With no signs or permits, she sells beer and fried food to friends and neighbors at tables on her patio.
She hugs me and welcomes me into the family I do not belong to.
She tells me David looks exactly like his daddy, her younger brother Ramón.
She tells me what a good man Ramón was, what a hard worker.
I sit with David and his tía at one of her wooden tables and she brings us beer.
She tells me how excited Ramón was about the baby coming, how he said he wanted a boy.
She brings us more beer.
It gets dark.
He would have gladly died for his country, but not like that.
She brings more beer.
David and la tía talk about David's father and both of them weep without shame.
Drinking and crying, drinking and crying.
They shot them against a wall in the morning sunshine.
Shot them and walked away.

A LUCKY BREATH

David's mother was six months pregnant.
Ramón was so excited for the arrival of his firstborn.
Times were tough and he wanted to be prepared, so he had already purchased a box of diapers.
Diapers.
The only thing he ever bought for his son.
La tía and David cry over the box of diapers.
High cheekbones, a thick lower lip, wide chocolate eyes, and a box of diapers.
I ask la tía where the bathroom is.
She says she has to go too, so she'll show me.
We walk around the corner of the house.
She says it's not a very nice bathroom, so sometimes she prefers just to go here in the garden.
I say that's alright with me.
I squat and pee with David's tía in the dark by the hibiscus.
She tells me David is a good man.
I say yes he is.
She says he is lucky to have me.

I say thank you and wish I had never been born.

In the beginning, she was nearly 100. She called mi "mi nieta" and wrapped her soft brown arms around me every time we met. Her name was Albertina. Los Ríos called her "Doña Tina." To us, she was "Abuelita."

Dona Tina was Martín's mother. She'd given birth to five sons and raised them, like many women of her time and place, without a husband. The Catholic priest preached sermons on the importance of marriage, but he wanted coins in exchange for it. Coins were rare in Los Ríos, difficult to obtain, and only exchanged for absolute necessities. Even the priest knew heaven's paper blessings were impossible in the villages.

I loved Abuelita's stories. She told of times when Los Ríos was a collection of a half dozen houses scattered beside a road to nowhere. The single-room wooden homes had thatched roofs, dirt floors, and a well outside. No one imagined electricity. No one had anything extra. They lived on the corn and beans they grew in the rainy season, milk and fresh cheese from their cows, platanos, eggs, and on special occasions, meat. Abuelita Tina made clay water pots and comales for cooking tortillas. She and her sisters balanced stacks of heavy clay comales on their heads and walked barefoot to Santa Cruz to sell them. It took the whole day to walk there and another day to walk back, but it was the only way they could earn money to buy coffee, sugar, matches to light a cooking fire, a piece of cloth for a dress. She remembered the long walks fondly. I asked her if walking 12 kilometers barefoot hurt her feet. She laughed and said no.

Abuelita Tina told me stories I wouldn't have dared to disbelieve. She told me about small evil-intentioned elf-like beings that lived in the forests and fields. They would try to trick curious children into following them away from their homes and then kidnap them never to return them. She told me about another evil spirit that changed forms. Sometimes it was a monkey, sometimes a beautiful woman. This wicked monkey woman's intent was to seduce men and steal them from their families. A noise in the night on the roof might mean she was there in monkey form, waiting. Abuelita Tina didn't laugh or smile about these things so neither did I. I could tell by the way she lowered her voice and told me to be careful that they were real.

"Leones" had once been a danger in Los Ríos, she said, meaning wildcats like jaguars and pumas. Women washing clothes in the stream that ran behind the plaza through the trees watched each other's backs while they worked. Lions were dangerous to the children that accompanied their young mothers to the water. The big cats were especially dangerous to pregnant women, Abuelita Tina told me, gravely, with wide eyes. They could sense an unborn child in the womb even before its mother suspected its existence, she said, and would approach stealthily, hungrily. A visit from a wildcat at the river was often the first sign a woman received that she was pregnant, Abuelita said. These magical and terrible felines knew these things, she said, and they were never wrong.

Enrique and I drove her in our car to see a doctor in Santa Cruz when her aches and pains needed attention. We drank hot coffee with her on some Sunday afternoons on the porch of her little house. She gave us lemons from her tree, and eggs to take home if her hens had been generous.

Her stories, eventually, lost their beginnings and ends, and melted into a litany of words and images. She loved telling stories even after she no longer remembered them, and the words added up to nothing more than syllables. Jesus, jaguars, childhood friends, the neighbor's chickens, and what we're going to eat for dinner all blended into a single glorious tale, and she wanted us to listen.

It's David's birthday.
Today, he is 21.
He wants to have a party, so we go to the market to buy food for a special meal.
We buy yucca, platanos, tomatoes, cabbage, onions, and pork for a soup called vajo.
We buy beer and lots of rum.
This is my last gift to him.
In two days, we will take a bus back to the border of Costa Rica, and part ways.
At the border, David will take a bus back to his life in Los Ríos.
I will take a bus to San José where my luggage and my plane tickets are waiting for me in a corner of the dining room of the house in Guadeloupe.

The soup is ready early.
We eat big bowls of it in the afternoon and wait for night.
Cousins and friends begin to arrive at dusk.
The endless soup and rum are enough for everyone.
We play music, drink, and laugh.
Night falls over Rivas.
We decide to go to the lake.

David, his stepfather José, a half dozen cousins, and I cram into the car that finally runs.
We drive to San Jorge to the shore of Lake Nicaragua.
The rum is with us, and we are drunk in the starry night.
We pile out of the car and sit on the beach with the cool lake wind on our faces, passing the bottle around.
The night is beautiful.

David asks me to stay with him in this enchanted country and to make our lie come true.
He asks me to marry him.
I look out over the infinite black lake and say I cannot.
My heart breaks a little when I say it.
David deserves happiness.
He has suffered enough sadness.
But I cannot give it to him.
David is drunk and now he is crying.
He is crying because he is in love with me and I am not in love with him.
He pleads with me.
I kiss him and say nothing.
The birthday party isn't fun anymore.
I wish I wasn't here.
I wish I was home.
I don't have a home.
I wish I was anywhere else but here, now, drunk with all these men.
Everyone is drunk, terribly drunk.
It's dark and David is crying.
He is getting angry.
He wants me to give him a reason why I won't marry him.
I can only say that I can't.

We drive back to Rivas, into the city center to buy food because we are too drunk.
The food stand is crowded with drunken men.
Fighting starts.
David and his cousins are in the middle of the fight.
They curse and kick and sling their fists, falling to the ground in their own clumsiness.
David's jeans are ripped and his knee is bleeding.

We decide to leave.
I am going to drive.
I am much too drunk to drive, but all the men are incoherent.
I can walk without stumbling.
I can think, if I concentrate.
I start the car and head slowly toward home, forcing my attention to the street.
David and José are in the front seat beside me.
Suddenly, they are fighting each other.
I don't know what they are fighting about.
They are shouting, shoving, and flailing fists at each other beside me.
They are so drunk even they don't know what they are fighting about.
I stop the car in the street and get out of the driver's seat.
I am afraid.
I have to get out right now.
Too many drunk men are too close together in this car.
I stand in the street beside the car with no idea what to do.
Everyone else gets out of the car too, except José who slams it into gear and drives away.
We walk for a long time.
I am tired.
David stumbles.
I think he will lie down in the street if I stop walking, so I don't stop.

A LUCKY BREATH

～∂∽

It's illegal to kill wild animals in Costa Rica, so what we did the night Enrique took me armadillo hunting with the men was a crime. Armadillo meat isn't delicious, but it is free. If you cook it long enough, change the water enough times, mince it finely, and add enough spices, it begins to taste alright. Women don't hunt armadillos, men do. Women cook them after men have carried them home dead and skinned them. But I asked so many questions the night Enrique brought home a rat-like armadillo carcass that he said the next time they all went hunting, I could come along. If I could keep up. I said no problem.

To catch an armadillo, you need dogs, a shovel, some flashlights, and a big stick. A half dozen of us climbed into the back of a pickup truck with Mateo and his dogs and took off out of Los Ríos into the hills. Armadillos are nocturnal, so the only time to catch them is at night. Moonlight makes finding the burrows easier for human eyes, so it's best to choose a night near the full moon.

We parked the truck on a hillside and Mateo let the dogs loose. They ran around in all directions, sniffing, snuffling, and yelping once in a while. We waited for them to scent a trail. Enrique asked me if I wanted to be the one to pull the armadillo out of its hole. I said yes. Mateo asked me if I wanted to kill it. I said no.

The night wind ruffled the grass at our feet, and the moonlight on the trees and shoulders of the men was beautiful. They gossiped and teased each other until wild barking signaled to us that one of the dogs had chased an armadillo into its burrow. We ran through the dry field as best we could in the shining dark, trying not to trip over rocks or step on snakes.

Mateo hushed the dogs and congratulated them, while one of the other men began digging away the dirt around the armadillo burrow the dogs discovered. Inside this dark den, we hoped, was a terrified animal we were going to eat. Enrique shone the flashlight into the hole, illuminating the tip of a tail. It was a huge armadillo.

The next thing that needed to happen was for someone to pull it out, and I had agreed to do it. Everyone shouted instructions at once, and I tried to follow them all. I planted my feet on either side of the partially-excavated den, squatted, and reached in. Breathless with revulsion and excitement, I took ahold of the snaky tail with both hands. I felt the creature I couldn't see stiffen, then scuffle frantically for an impossible escape. I screamed but I didn't let go. The men shouted for me to pull.

I pulled as hard as I could, and the armadillo held its ground. It didn't budge. I leaned my weight against it and pulled with my whole body. I didn't want to fail at this challenge. The armadillo, somehow, did not move. Enrique turned away, making disgusted gestures in the air, saying I wouldn't be able to do it. I needed to prove him wrong.

I pulled on the tail of the terrified animal until its grip faltered and it began to move toward me. I pulled, stepped backward, pulled some more. Our friends cheered and shouted, ordering me not to let it go. Mateo told me to be careful or it would bite me, but he was laughing, and I laughed too.

Its little legs scratched desperately, trying to get back into the dark when I dragged the armadillo from the earth into the moonlight. The dogs went insane. I was sweating and my hands were raw from this small dinosaur's scaley tail. Enrique stepped up and took over, grabbing the armadillo roughly and cursing cheerfully at it, beaming at his friends. He was proud of me.

I was proud of me too, but I knew what would happen next was something I didn't want to watch. I turned around and looked at the moon-lit trees waving their hands.

The next day I minced the smelly meat, boiled it three times in lemon water, then sautéed it with plenty of onion, cilantro, and *sweet pepper. Enrique was proud of that too. It tasted pretty good with enough tabasco sauce, but I was happy that he shared it with Mateo and the others.*

The day comes when I must leave Nicaragua, leave David, and return to my country with my suitcases.
David and I ride the bus together to the border.
He holds my hand but cannot look at me.
He refuses to believe I will leave him.
He tells me that I will abandon my plans and stay.
I cannot speak.
I have nothing to say.
I am only doing what I said from the beginning I would do.
It is time.

We cross the border, the stamps slammed into our passports.
It feels unreal, like a dream.
I am trembling.
I don't know why.
I will take a bus to San José, spend the night with Rebeca's family, and get on a plane in the morning.
I am ready.
I just want this to be over.

David says he's not going back to Los Ríos.
He says he can't live there without me.
He says Enrique will stalk him.
He says instead, he will go to the port city called Puntarenas where he has cousins.
They can find him a job in the tuna processing plants.
We hug.
Kiss, again and again.
Say goodbye
Then I am on the bus in my seat waiting for it to pull away from the dirty border station.

I am happy.
I am numb.
I am nothing.
The life I wanted is gone.
Everything is over.
No one is left to say goodbye to.

When the bus engine starts, the door flies open and David is climbing up the steps.
Tears stream down his beautiful cheeks.
My heart freezes, melts.
What is he doing?

David rides with me to San José, holding on to me as if I will keep him from drowning.
He doesn't care that he will have to take a bus back to Puntarenas tomorrow.
These last hours together are worth it, he says.
Then our bus arrives at the terminal in San José and we must say goodbye again.

By now it is night.
We stand on the street with our backpacks.
The rest of the city thunders around us as if nothing were happening.
As if it didn't matter that we have been glorious lovers and we will never see each other again.
David waits for me to break, say I can't leave him, that I won't go.
I can't breathe.
I kiss him and get in a taxi.
I am already broken.

The next morning in the cold of Rebeca's house, the telephone rings.
It's David.
He says he wants to see me off at the airport.
I tell him what time the flight is because I can't think of anything else to say.
David arrives at the airport.
He waits at the gate with me.
He tells me he has spent all of his money and has no way to get to his cousin's home in Puntarenas.
He has nothing to begin his new life with, and I know it.
I give him a hundred dollars.
I don't know what else to do.
When I board the plane, he is crying.
I am not.
My body is full of cold ashes.

A LUCKY BREATH

There is a place in the world called El Silencio. Going southwest through Los Ríos, and after the cemetery, if you turn right on the road through the field and press up the mountain that the sun sets behind, you will find it. It isn't a town; you won't see it on a map. But it is there—a fistful of houses scattered on the mountainside above Los Ríos along the dusty road. I only went twice to El Silencio—the evening Enrique took me to visit his aunt who lives there, and once years later to be sure it was real.

It is real.

Martín's sister-in-law lived in El Silencio. Her house in El Silencio was made of wood, set between a tin roof and a dirt floor. Enrique took me there one evening in our new car. He loved showing off his car and his American wife. I loved being with Enrique, being part of his world. Enrique's aunt and her house in El Silencio seemed like pieces lost from a fairytale. Imagine—a place so quiet it is named after silence. We sat at the wooden table in the kitchen on crooked wooden stools and drank sweet black coffee. The wooden-shuttered window stood open to the dry summer tree branches and stars. Wind roared and whirled the branches around, mussed our hair and annoyed the hens perched in the jocote tree.

Although I grew up on a chicken farm, it wasn't until I lived in Los Ríos that I learned that chickens like to sleep in trees. They hop and flutter up the rungs of a wooden ladder at dusk and settle onto their perches in jocote trees where the family dog can keep them safe from iguanas and coons while they sleep. They teach this to their chicks. This is life in Los Ríos. This life in El Silencio.

I loved Enrique for belonging to this, for being something elemental and real. Over and over, I forgave him: for shouting, for grumbling, for insults, for insensitivities, for the time he nearly suffocated me on the couch. I loved him for his authenticity—for *the purity of his raw humanness. Nothing about Enrique ever involved pretense. Accuse him of anything but that.*

Sitting at a rough-hewn table in the circle of light from a bare bulb in a silent place called El Silencio drinking hot sugared coffee with Enrique's soft-spoken aunt, we are in a place before or after Time. A place far away from the world outside of the circle of light. Everything here is connected, is essential. The walls around us are made out of the trees over our heads that grow out of the dirt of the floor under our feet.

In El Silencio, I understand something I cannot explain about the meaning of being a human, alive on a planet among other living things.

Part IV: Atlanta

It's cold in Atlanta.
It's the beginning of May.
My sister Michelle lives here in a house with her husband and their dog.
Michelle and her husband have jobs, and she goes to grad school.

I've always heard that Atlanta is hot, but I am cold.
I can't feel my fingers or my toes.
I wear sweaters and long pants even though everyone else is wearing shorts and tank tops.
I sit on the floor in the patch of sun even though there are couches and chairs.
The floor has carpet.
I forgot about carpet.
It seems strange and somehow unsanitary.
The house has an extra bedroom that no one sleeps in.
I put my suitcases here and now it is mine.
I open the suitcases and hang my clothes in the closet.

I'm cold.
I can't sleep at night because the house is too quiet.
The rooms are shut like coffins.
No sounds come from outside: no crickets, no frogs, no roosters on the hour.
The windows are closed and the silence of the walls is deafening.
My own breathing is so loud in the dark that I cannot sleep.
It seems the rest of the world has disappeared and I am the only living thing in it.

The bathroom has hot water.
The refrigerator is full of delicacies like cheese, lettuce, and beer.
There are plates and silverware for everyone, and for people who are not here but who could someday come to visit.
I can do anything I want, and no one will shout at me, ever.
Ever.
No one will call me stupid or lazy like Enrique did, even though we both knew it wasn't true.
I do nothing all afternoon and no one even notices.

There is a computer here.
It has its own room.
The computer sits in its room on a table by a window.
I sit at the computer and look for jobs.
I sit at the computer and look out the window.
Outside is a yard for the dog.
There is grass, and the grass is green.
A cow would like it.
The sky is gray.
The grass is green, and it moves in the breeze.
There are green trees with their roots down in the cold dirt and their leaves up in the cold sky.

A LUCKY BREATH

There must be wind.
I can't hear it or feel it, but I see the leaves and grass move.
The window is closed and the wind is outside.
I am inside.
Outside.
Inside.
Two separate worlds.
I open the window to feel the wind, to hear something like maybe a bird.
I want to smell the grass.
But the wind is cold and I don't hear any birds.
I don't hear anything.
I don't smell anything.
I want to walk outside to feel the grass and dirt with my feet, but the grass is cold and the dirt is cold.
The sun is shining but nothing is warm.
I sit at the computer and search for jobs, jobs for someone who can speak Spanish and doesn't know what to do.
I find some that might be alright.
Now, I have to make a resume and list references.
I write emails to my college professors and past employers from before I ever went to Los Ríos.
The last time they heard from me, I said I would leave and never come back.
I write them letters to tell them I came back.

I am terribly sleepy.
I wish I never had to wake up.
I make some coffee, but the coffee here tastes funny.
I am still sleepy.
But at least the cup is warm.
A little life flows back into my frozen fingers, so I type some more.

I think, "I am free."
No one will shout at me.
Enrique can sleep with whomever he wants and no one will look at me with pity behind their smiles.
No one will be drunk and breaking windows when I come home.
I don't have to buy things for David or his family.
I don't have to fix anyone's car that won't start.
No one is trying to make me be anything.
I don't feel free.
I feel lost.

A LUCKY BREATH

We'd been married for six months when Enrique hurt me. It happened on the day we moved from the little house in Santa Cruz back to Los Ríos. While I unpacked our bags and boxes in what would be our home for a few months, Enrique took off for the cantina where decent women aren't invited. I spent the evening sulkily settling in by myself. I thought he was just having a beer with the boys, so I wasn't prepared for him to come home devastatingly drunk, in a tornado of hilarity and fury.

This was new to me. I had only ever seen Enrique's happy drunk side—dancing, giggles, and a toothy grin. There was the bar brawl while I was gone at Christmas, but I hadn't seen it so I didn't have to think about it. I thought it was a one-time thing. I had not imagined what could happen to Enrique when he drank too much, how out of control he could become, what he might be capable of. Past a certain point, Enrique vanished and an insane man took his place.

He walked into the house that night without saying a word, turned on the TV, and sat on the couch. I asked if he'd had fun. He grunted. I offered him food, because he'd missed dinner. He shouted that he didn't want food.

He wanted to fight. He wanted to laugh, although nothing was funny. I sat on the couch beside him. Of course his wife was supposed to be angry at him for coming home drunk, but instinct told me to avoid upsetting him. I was more hurt by his absence than angry about his condition, so I pretended not to notice. I hoped that if he saw I wasn't angry with him, he would stop glaring at me, trying to pick a fight. He grabbed me then, and kissed me roughly until it hurt. I pulled away from him. He crushed me against him and bit my face. The more I protested, the tighter he held me, so that the less I struggled, the better.

Enrique stood up from the couch and flung the cushions he was sitting on onto the floor. He pushed me so I would stand up, then he pushed the rest of the cushions onto the floor. He wanted me to fight him, to shout at him for that, but I didn't. He was scaring me. I didn't know who he was. I was afraid to walk away, so I sat down on the bare couch frame.

Enrique sat beside me, took a cushion from the floor, and pushed it at me. The gesture felt threatening, but I tried to pretend we were playing. I laughed and held up my hands. He pushed harder. I forced myself to laugh more. He pushed harder and glared at me. I stopped laughing, stopped resisting, and let him push me down with the cushion. He pushed me down onto the bare couch until my face was pressed flat against the bottom of it by the cushion in his hands. Then Enrique grabbed a handful of my long hair and pulled. He kept pushing down on my head with the couch cushion. And he continued pulling my hair. I told him he was hurting me. I told him I couldn't breathe. He snarled something unintelligible, pressed down on me with his full weight, and yanked my hair.

I understood in that moment that this man wasn't my husband. Whoever he was, this man was capable of killing me. I turned my face to the side where the tiniest bit of light and air reached me at a spot that the cushion didn't touch the couch frame, and I stopped fighting. I played dead. Through the searing pain in my scalp and the agony of my twisted neck, I kept still.

Enrique pushed down on me. Just a little more and my neck will snap, I thought, or the tiny air hole will be covered and I will suffocate here on my couch in my new house, murdered by my husband who has gone insane and forgotten that he loves me.

Once, in a college musical production, the character I played had to die on stage and lie there dead while the other characters finished singing the song. It seemed like a hundred years ago. I'd had to practice breathing for that scene in a way that no one would notice the movement of my chest. I remembered that death scene that night on the couch with Enrique's weight pressing on my chest and neck. I tried to breathe invisibly the same way I had on stage, and willed the hair to tear from my head. I focused with all my might on the tiny crack of light, the tiny whisp of air, and waited.

After I became silent and still as death, Enrique let me up. I held back the tears that wanted to spill because now, more than disappointment, anger, or pain, I was overwhelmed by fear.

The next day there was a tender welt on my scalp where the hair refused to let go, and I couldn't turn my head to the right. Lying in bed nursing the hangover, Enrique noticed my awkward movements and asked what was the matter with me. I asked him if he remembered throwing the pillows off the couch. He said no. I asked him if he remembered pulling my hair or pushing me down. He said no.

I told him what he did to me, how he suffocated me and pulled my hair. He said it wasn't true. I made him touch the lump on my head. He shrugged then, giggled sheepishly, and said he didn't remember leaving the bar.

Enrique wasn't a bad man. He was a wonderful friend and an irresistible lover. But he was a complicated husband and a dangerous drunk.

Zimmerman

When no one is home and it is dark, I go outside and pee in the grass behind the house in Atlanta.
Like I did so many times in Costa Rica.
Like I did so many times in Nicaragua.
Here, this is illegal.
They will fine me if they catch me.
No one will catch me.
All the windows no one ever looks out of in the houses where strangers live are covered by thick curtains.
Porches and patios have beautiful empty chairs.

My parents fly from Pennsylvania to visit us.
They're so happy to see me, they almost can't remember to be sorry for my dead marriage.
My invisible life.
They assure me that I've done the right thing and that everything will be alright.
I say of course it will.
But I don't know what that means.
I don't understand "alright."
Nothing is alright.
Everything is in tiny pieces that don't fit together.

Michelle introduces me to her friends.
They are funny, smart, and friendly.
We go out for beer.
"I just moved here from Costa Rica," I tell them.
"Oh, so you're the sister from Costa Rica!" they exclaim.
"What made you decide to leave?" they ask.
"I decided I want to go to grad school," I tell them.

"That's great," they say.
"For what?" they ask.
Grad school isn't like college: you don't just go and then figure out what you want to be.
I don't know what I want to be.
I wanted to live in Costa Rica where I am never cold.
Here, I am always cold.
I say, "Creative writing," and everyone thinks that's very nice.

Michelle and I go for runs during the cold spring mornings.
When we come home from our runs my forehead is humid but my ears are numb and red.
My nose is ice.
I catch a cold and stop running.

We go to parties.
We go to church.
Everyone is friendly.
Everyone is curious.
Everyone asks me a lot of questions, but I've forgotten all the answers.
I don't remember anything.
Everyone asks me what I want to do and I don't know what to say.
I don't remember why I came here.
I used to know, but I don't anymore.
All I can remember is David and the twist of his upper lip when he smiles.
I see the color of the veranera growing in front of María's house.
I hear the roosters that crow every hour of the day and night.
I feel the warm salt ocean on my skin and the hot sun like an iron flattening my body.
I remember Enrique riding up to the house on his bicycle with

the toothy grin of a good day.
I don't know a single song on the radio.

Michelle takes me shopping because I don't have any clothes I can wear to a job interview.
My only shoes are flip-flops and old sneakers.
I buy gray pants, white shirts, blue skirts, a beige jacket, and black flats so I can look like everyone.
Like no one.

I apply for a job with a church agency that assists "the poor."
That seems like a good job for me.
I think I would fit in—if not with the people who pay me, at least with the clientele.
We would understand each other, I think.
I don't really like calling people without enough money "the poor," but I can live with it.
Poor people know they're poor so they don't mind it if you say they are.

They call me for an interview.
I put on some of my serious new clothes and drive to the office without getting lost.
I sit at a table with kind-hearted church people in a room with a lot of windows.
They tell me all about the job.
They tell me about "the poor."
I try to imagine myself in black flats and nylon stockings somehow helping poor people, but I get confused.
When they ask me why I want to help "the poor," words fly away from me and I see only pictures.
I see Enrique getting off the bus in Belen with everything he owns in the green backpack.

I see María patting out tortillas of hand-ground corn.
I see little Miguel beaming in well-shined hand-me-down school shoes.
The piles of hair I cut two weeks ago in the Nicaraguan shade.
David's little sisters eating rice with new spoons.
Manduko carrying my bathwater.
Blood on the wall behind David's daddy and his brothers, dead in the morning sunshine.
All of the sudden, right there in my job interview, I'm going to cry.
They aren't "the poor."
They're my people, my family.
I don't want to help them.
I want to be with them.
I don't know how to live without them.
I can't answer the question.
My mouth won't cooperate.
They wait for me to say something and they see I am going to cry.
I can't even say I'm sorry.
I can see them wondering what is wrong with me.
Finally, someone asks me something else.
The church people thank me kindly and I don't get the job.

I sign up with a temporary employment agency.
They give me tests that I do extremely well on.
They say they don't understand why I am applying with their agency.
They think I should apply for a real job.
I have a college degree and I speak two languages.
I don't know what to say for myself, but at least this time I don't think of Manduko carrying water.
This time I don't cry.

When they call me with an offer, it's to dress up as a hamburger who interviews customers at Burger King.
I say I can't make it, and mail more resumes.

A LUCKY BREATH

Traveling from Santa Cruz to Playa Celeste every day with a combination of buses and hitchhiking was unreliable and took a long time. I wasn't afraid to thumb a ride, but obvious dangers exist. Hitchhiking was a common method of travel in Guanacaste, then. I met a lot of people that way, learned the names of towns, rivers, trees, and heard the stories of many strangers. I told my story more times than I wanted to. It worked well enough, but it was no way to live.

When I looked into my crystal ball, I saw myself pregnant someday soon. Was I going to stand by the road waiting for a ride with a baby in my belly? What about afterward? I couldn't imagine simply not working for years on end. Neither could I see myself, as a mother, hitchhiking back and forth to work every day. For some reason that seemed wrong to me, perilous and absurd.

I asked my parents in a letter if they would lend me money for a little car. I told them I wouldn't have to hitchhike every day that way, and that I would pay them back. I was sure I could do it if the car was cheap enough and they were patient.

I could have gotten a job right in Santa Cruz where we lived, but I made better money at the coast, and I liked the connection to the international community. It was easily worth the investment of a car. On weekends, Enrique and I could go to Los Ríos together without having to pay a taxi or call someone to come pick us up. Grocery shopping on Saturdays would be much easier in a car than on a bicycle with a backpack so heavy I could barely swing it onto my back.

My parents said yes.

We went to San José on the bus to buy the car, and I drove it home in it. Enrique didn't know how to drive, so in the following weeks, I taught him. The purpose of the car was to get me to work, but of course I wanted Enrique to be able to drive it. He was so wildly delighted, like a kid on Christmas Eve. He'd never imagined he would have the luck of owning a car, and now one sat outside the house in the yard, all ours. He got the hang of driving quickly. And then there were urgent errands to run and favors to do for friends every time I walked through the door and he heard the keys hit the table.

Whereas I'd felt sad when the new TV captured Enrique's attention in his free time, now I felt lucky when he was home. With the car, we didn't need to live in Santa Cruz anymore for me to get to work each day, so we moved back to Los Ríos.

One of our sisters-in-law offered us her grandmother's house. Grandmother wasn't living there anymore, and neither was anyone else for the moment. A cousin from San José planned to fix it up and move in someday, but no one knew when that day would be. The family was grateful to have it occupied, the grass cut, and the electricity paid. They wouldn't have let us pay them money if we had tried.

The house was an old Guanacaste-style house, with a cement floor, a tin roof, and wooden walls that leaves would slip through on windy days. The windows were shuttered eyes that we opened in the morning to the sun and the free air, and closed at night when we went to bed. Indoors, the kitchen faucet was the only running water. The shower was a tin enclosure on the back patio under the blue sky.

Mateo and Norma were our next-door-neighbors, which was both wonderful and complicated. Norma couldn't be mad at us anymore since we'd gotten married, but it wasn't easy for her to put her self-righteousness away.

Half way across the yard, stood our outhouse. There were still enough homes in rural Costa Rica with outhouses that general stores sold chamber pots. Enrique bought one and insisted that I set it in the corner of our bedroom each night so that I wouldn't *have to go outside in the dark to pee. I said I wasn't scared, but he put his foot down. He said it was dangerous, that I might step on a snake or meet up with a dead person. I laughed and said alright.*

I loved that house. It felt like it had grown up out of the ground like a Guanacaste tree. It belonged in the space it took up. Everyone called it "fea" because it was old with warped boards for walls, no glass in the windows, and no toilet. I didn't care. I thought it was beautiful. It was my dream house—simple and essential—a house to be born or to die in.

Letters come to Atlanta from Enrique.
They are gut-wrenching love letters full of agony and pleading.
In the first letter, he swears it isn't true.
No matter what anyone says, Enrique insists, it isn't true that he and Jennifer went to the river together on Sunday.
So, I should come home.
What Jennifer? I think.
What river?
You mean that last Sunday afternoon?
Before the dance we went to?
Or a different Sunday?
I'd never heard anything about a Jennifer or a river until he backwardly confessed it in that letter.
But it doesn't matter anymore.
I'm safe on the other side.
His begging and his lovely lies do not move me.
More letters come.
They are beautiful and terrible, containing more of his presence than entire years we spent sleeping in the same bed.
He promises me everything if I will come back.
He is a changed man, he says.
Come home and see for yourself.
I know that he believes it even if I cannot.

Letters come from Angel.
Reports on the family, the children, the story that two weeks after I left, Enrique brought another woman to live with him in our house.
Two weeks.
I wasn't even in Nicaragua, then.

A LUCKY BREATH

I knew he had "women," but I never imagined this one.
The daughter of a family who lives near his workshop.
A little girl.
Maybe 16.
Never once did I think.
I suspected he visited the house because of her mother.
I'd never thought to be jealous of the little girl.
Now he has moved this woman-child into my house with him.
But continues to write me these letters full of heartbreaking lies.
I do not care that the girl is there with him.
It's just as well that Enrique has found himself a companion.
I am never coming back.

I stopped taking birth control pills and waited for the unimaginable, for the day I would not get my period because I was pregnant.

I had very much wanted not to be pregnant before we were married. Not because of my personal religious convictions, but because of those of my parents. It seemed like one heartache I could spare them. The wedding dissolved that obstacle with nothing more than a signature and, at 26, I decided the moment had come. There was the question of whether or not we could provide for a child, but I didn't bother Enrique with that. The question doesn't translate across cultures.

Nothing happened. But that's normal, at first. I'd been on and off birth control pills for several years, so I didn't expect to be pregnant immediately. I didn't really want to be pregnant immediately. A little time to get mentally ready suited me fine.

More time went by. Still nothing happened. Whereas once the first pangs of what was going to be my cycle brought infinite relief, now they brought a wave of disappointment. But what's there to do? Wait. Keep waiting.

Enrique asked me what was wrong with me and told me if I was barren, he would have children with someone else. I pretended I thought he was making a not-funny joke even though I expected he wasn't. I thought about telling him the next time he said something like that I would start taking pills again, but I decided that was a bad idea.

Months passed.

Nothing.

"When are you going to have a baby?" people asked me. "What's wrong? Can't you have children? Don't you like children?"

A healthy young woman in her twenties, especially if she has a husband, is supposed to be pregnant or have a child or both. Otherwise, something is wrong. There is no other explanation.

I managed always to be gracious. The question and its manner of phrasing, no matter how much it annoyed or injured me, comes from a love for children. And a desire to connect. Having children would make me a member of the family, the town, the country, in a new and deeper way. The person asking this would be imagining our children starting school together. And our grandchildren. My daughter perhaps marrying his or her son. Etcetera. There was never an iota of contempt in the question. I sometimes sensed sympathy—clearly, I must be suffering from either a physical problem or a mental one.

But nothing happened.

I decided it was time to see a doctor.

The Costa Rican national health care system is free, but the processes are lugubrious. Having more time than money, I didn't mind. Normally, to get an appointment for non-emergent treatment, I would have had to go to Santa Cruz in the dark of early morning to stand in line. But thankfully a neighbor who worked in the office took my little yellow appointment card to work with her and reserved a visit for me.

The doctor gave me a general physical, noted my concern, and referred me for an appointment with a gynecologist. The next available appointment was in three months. I hoped by that time I wouldn't need the appointment.

Three months later I saw a gynecologist for a routine exam. A month after that, I returned for an appointment to learn that the results showed nothing out of the ordinary, and I, still not pregnant, was referred to the hospital in Nicoya for an ultrasound. In another three months. The gynecologist patiently explained the female reproductive cycle and how to determine when I was ovu-

lating. I didn't mention that I already know this. I didn't bother explaining that for me to tell Enrique when to have sex would be, rather than a help to conception, an excellent form of birth control. Sex was only allowed to be Enrique's idea. I had tried to explain ovulation to him months ago, to which he snorted, "Solo babosadas," and told me if I weren't machorra I would be pregnant by now. There wasn't much room for argument, there. We both knew perfectly well he wasn't the problem.

The ultrasound showed a slightly backward-tilting uterus but, the doctor explained, this is common and does not inhibit conception. Everything revealed itself to be in the right place and in perfect condition. The doctor gave me a special sheet on which to record my body temperature each hour of the day and told me to make an appointment after I'd filled out three months of temperature sheets.

I dropped it. I bought a thermometer and took my temperature a few times, but I never made the next appointment. Either I would get pregnant, or I wouldn't.

There wasn't a lot of use I kept taking my temperature multiple times a day, trying to pin down the exact moment of ovulation, if Enrique was going to blow me off and laugh at me. And maybe, just maybe, I didn't want to have children with him anyway. Maybe we were better this way, just us. He already had children both of us could love. I would have liked to have one of my own, but perhaps I should leave good enough alone, I reasoned. If Enrique couldn't take me seriously and be even a little bit supportive, trying to raise a child together must be a spectacularly terrible idea.

A LUCKY BREATH

❦

I ride the bus downtown.
I love the bus.
On the bus the people look at you.
They see what you are, not what they think you should be.
They ask you things like where you're getting off the bus, or, "How are you doing today?"
They don't ask you why.
They don't ask what you're going to do tomorrow.
They don't ask how the job search is going.
Or where you want to go to grad school.
Nobody on the bus ever asks me anything I don't know the answer to.
They say they like my coat, and am I cold?
I say yes I am.
It is almost June.
They say, "Have a good day."

I go to the Coca-Cola Museum.
There are rooms full of things to look at.
Nobody in the Coca-Cola Museum asks me anything at all.
A big-screen slideshow depicts Coca-Cola being sold all over the world.
There's a picture of a Latino man standing in the mountains wearing a campesino hat.
Perhaps it is Ecuador?
Peru?
He smiles widely with no front teeth.
Behind him, a Coca-Cola truck is driving along a dirt road bringing Coke to people like him who live nowhere.
Everybody in the audience laughs.
This picture is very funny.

I start to cry, because the man looks like Enrique's Tío Filo.
Tío Filo, who built us a crooked car port of thin tree trunks and tin when we bought the truck.
Tio Filo, who always hugged me and proudly crowed, "Mi sobrina!"
I remember how he wailed the day he buried his oldest son.
I never even said goodbye to him.

I go into a shopping plaza and buy some Atlanta postcards.
Three of them.
One for each of the children.
I buy a styrofoam cup of coffee and sit at a little fast-food table with a pen I brought in my purse and the post cards.
I write Querida Carina María on one, but I don't know what else to say.
What do you write on a postcard to a six-year-old girl?
One that you walked away from one day while she was in kindergarten?
What can you possibly say to her?
Just yesterday, I was teaching her to write letters in a notebook at my kitchen table.
She said she wanted to be a teacher, like me.
I remember the first time I held her.
She was two.
She fell asleep in my arms while we waited for her papá.
Querido Miguel.
Remember when my parents came to visit, and you drank a whole cup of bitter black coffee because my mom forgot to offer sugar, and you were too shy to ask?
Wasn't that hilarious?
Querido Adán.
Remember the time you got so sunburned we had to cover you in cucumber slices?

A LUCKY BREATH

You were lying there crying but you looked so funny we couldn't help but laugh.
Remember the time we brought that truckful of platanos back from Guapiles, and then your daddy wasn't in the mood to them?
Remember how I had to do it for him, and he made you help me?
We drove down every road we came to until not one platano was left in the truck.
Remember how you hugged me and told me not to cry the day your daddy got drunk and broke the bedroom windows?

What do you write to your children on a bunch of stupid postcards?
I didn't say goodbye to anyone.
I want to cut my hands and send them my blood.
I write something that I hope is cheerful and affectionate, and I get up from the table without drinking the horrible mall coffee.

Enrique's power games started almost as soon as we married. The first ones were small. He would do things like take a bite out of a baguette, toss it on the table, and walk away, or open the refrigerator and eat jelly from the jar with a spoon. When I asked him to put the bread back in the bag or not to eat the jelly with a spoon, he would snarl at me, then punish me for hours with angry silence. At first, I felt bad. I tried to make my suggestions more kindly, even though I knew I hadn't been mean. I wanted him to be happy and I assumed he wanted the same for me. I would have done anything not to offend him.

He started calling me stubborn, stupid. If I said something he didn't like or want to believe, he called me a liar. If I arrived home from work later than he did, he greeted me gruffly and threatened to make me stay home. Women who came home late from work weren't to be trusted out of the house. I pretended that this didn't bother me.

One morning after he finished drinking his coffee, Enrique blankly informed me that if he wanted to, he would throw the mug against the ceramic floor. It was my favorite mug and he knew it. "Lo hago si quiero," he said. We weren't even having a fight; he just upset me for something to do. I didn't understand. But I knew it was a test, a challenge, and that if I displayed distress or love toward my mug, he would shatter it. To hurt me.

"Yo lo sé," I said back as stoically as possible. "Hágalo."

"Lo hago," he threatened.

"Ok," I said.

He didn't do it. But he wasn't lying. He would have done something to hurt me just to show me he could. I was stunned. I would never have done that.

It gets worse.
I can't listen to music because it makes me cry.
All of it.
I can't watch TV because I hate it.
I hate the sound of it.
It's fake and unbearably stupid.
Movies make me cry like music does.
All movies.
I don't like going to church with Michelle anymore because the songs there make me cry, too.
The Bible verses make me cry and the sermons make me cry.
It doesn't matter what they say.
People recognize me now and ask me friendly questions.
How am I doing?
How is the job search going?
How do I like this wonderful weather?
Do I hear from my friends in Costa Rica?
What was it that I did there?
Mission work?
I am terrified of questions.
They want to be nice to me.
I want to be invisible.

I take a blanket and go to the park.
I spread the cold blanket on the cold grass and lie on it staring at the trees.
The trees are liars.
I hate these lying trees.
How can they live here?
They stand there, beautiful and green as if everything were fine.

Everything is not fine.
The sky in the city is gray, not blue.
The sun is cold, not warm.
Night isn't even dark—there are always lights.
These trees have never seen night.
They have never heard silence.
Ever.
What do they know?
They have leaves and roots but they aren't real trees.
The grass isn't real and the sun isn't real.
The real sun is hot.
It can burn you through your clothes, melt your shoes as you walk along the road from Santa Cecilia.
This sun is cold.
Bright and cold.
Where am I?
Where are the real things?

A young couple that I met in Costa Rica lives here in Atlanta.
I call them on the phone.
They have a baby girl named Stella, and they want a babysitter who will talk to her in Spanish.
After all, she was conceived in Costa Rica.
I tell them I'm still job hunting, so I can work around their schedule.
They pay me too much money because they intuit that I need it.
I admit to them that I'm lost.
"Why don't you go back?" they ask me.
After I have come all the way here? I want to say.
After I burned all my bridges by running away to Nicaragua with David?
Go back to what?

A LUCKY BREATH

After only a month?
Where will I go?
What will I do?
What about grad school, the career, and the satisfying middle-class life I was going to have?
What if I fall in love with some other man who is just as bad as Enrique?
Or worse?
Michelle will never forgive me.
My parents will be destroyed.
"Go back," they say. "Go home."
But I don't know if I can.
I don't know anything.
I have nothing.
This is my chance.
If I go back, my chance is over.
If I don't go to grad school now, I never will.
Never is a long time.
I don't know if I want that.
I don't know what I want.

On one of January's scorching afternoons in 1997, Enrique and I got married in our living room in Santa Cruz. My best friend Beth and her husband flew from Wisconsin where they were in grad school to spend a week with us and to sign as our legal witnesses.

We didn't buy special wedding clothes. We'd spent all the money we had on the lawyer, two wedding bands, and the food and drink for our party. Enrique's parents came to the simple ceremony even though Enrique and Martín had spoken very little since the night Inez hit me and the whole family got involved. They brought Adán, and one of Enrique's brothers and his wife. Including Beth, her husband, and the lawyer who arrived two hours late, there were ten of us.

When I walked to the public phone to call the lawyer to ask where he was, he tried to cancel. I told him he had to come, even just for a minute, because our witnesses were waiting and our party guests would soon arrive. He rushed in two hours after our agreed time, sweating, and installed himself in front of us in our living room. He asked if we would like him to say a few words before we signed our names below the document inscribed into the book lying open on our little table. We said no thank you, but stood politely dripping sweat as he delivered a treatise on love and commitment that lasted almost an hour.

We were so happy. I felt glorious as we bent down to sign that book, like I was doing the impossible and knocking it out of the park. I felt like Christopher Columbus proving to all the doubters that the world isn't flat after all. Enrique beamed at me like the summer sun.

That night Enrique and I threw ourselves a party. We'd paid Mateo's mother to cook 20 hens in a giant cauldron for us over her fire. We bought beer, wine, Coca-Cola, and bottles of rum. Our friends from Los Ríos, Playa Celeste, and neighbors from up and down the street arrived with gifts and congratulations. One of them brought a pretty sheet cake with our names written on it in colored icing. We ate chicken and cake, drank beer and rum, turned our little radio/cassette player up loud, and danced in the living room.

I bought film for the camera so we would have pictures. There's one of Enrique and me standing nervously in front of the lawyer in our living room. There's a shot of us posing with little Adán on the front steps of our house. There's me beaming as the next-door neighbor hugs me. Sticky-fingered people eating chicken and tortillas. A pyramid of beer-logged laughing men on the back porch. My American girlfriends from Playa Celeste lined up on our donated couch. Beth hugging me. Enrique and me cutting the cake together through incapacitating giggles. Enrique and me feeding each other cake. Enrique and me with cake on our faces. It was the best day of my 26 years.

Later in the night, after a lot of beer and rum, we piled into a car and went to a dance at a town nearby. I remember the dark dance floor, Enrique spinning me until I almost fell, being tired, thinking this is my wedding day, this is my life, and being deliriously happy. I remember feeling like a queen. I don't remember going home.

We didn't go on a honeymoon. It isn't something we ever discussed or considered. Honeymoons were a thing rich people did, or people in movies. They didn't exist in our reality. We gave Beth and her husband our bed, as custom prescribed, and Enrique and I slept, the week we were married, on a mattress on the floor in our extra room.

The next day was a Sunday. Beth, her husband, Enrique, and I got up and onto a bus with our hangovers. We went to Playa Celeste to swim in the ocean, walk in the sun, eat fried fish and drink cold beer. Monday we were back at work wearing our new rings.

Things changed, then. Not immediately, but starting then. It wasn't the vows or the rings that caused a slow metamorphosis—it was the money. Both my parents and my grandparents gave us wedding gifts of money. It wasn't a lot of money, but it was a lot of money to us. With it, we bought the three appliances that changed our lives: a washer, a refrigerator, and a television.

The washer made weekends less burdensome for me. The small machine only did half of what an automatic washer does, but it took out most of the scrubbing and all the wringing that I needed to do by hand.

The refrigerator changed the way we shopped and ate. We shopped at actual supermarkets, not just neighborhood pulperías, and bought things that we didn't expect to finish within 12 or 24 hours. Our diets improved.

But it was the TV that brought the biggest change. From the day we brought it home there were no more long, dark, hot nights together lying on the bed talking and listening to the radio on the windowsill. After that, the moment Enrique got home from work, he sat in front of the TV and gave it his attention. If I wanted to be with him, I could join. And I did. Every night. And we sat in silence with our eyes on the screen until sleepiness took me away and left Enrique there in the fluorescent glare.

A LUCKY BREATH

༄

Michelle buys me a gift.
It's a ticket to go with her to an Indigo Girls concert.
I love the Indigo Girls, but I don't want to go to the concert because I know the music will make me cry.
All music makes me cry.
I go anyway.

At the concert, something happens to me.
The moment the music starts, I'm choking back tears and not doing a very good job of it.
I am losing the battle to a terrifying flood.
Because I had a life and I walked away from it.
I had so much love, and now I have none.
I had a husband, even though he was mean to me.
Was it my fault?
I wish it was my fault.
If it was my fault, I could fix it.
I had children.
I had beautiful lover who begged me not to leave.
He would have done anything to keep me, but there was nothing he could do.
I wanted to come here, alone, to this cold foreign country where everyone lives in silent boxes, and even at night it is never dark.
I wanted classes, books, a house with a computer in its own room, and black flats to wear to work.
I wanted to live here in America, but now that I'm here I don't remember why.
I thought I wanted this life, but now that it is in my hand, I don't.

Which country is my country?
What is my life?

I look around the space at all the people.
All the lesbian couples.
I haven't noticed lesbian couples on my bus rides through Atlanta, but I see them here.
They are doing what all couples do: holding hands, helping each other with jackets, a hand on the back so you don't stumble.
Living their lives in the way that's right for them.
No matter who else likes it or doesn't.
No matter who else gets it or does not.
No matter who smiles or frowns.
No matter who had other expectations for them.
Being happy.
Being themselves.

Envy stabs me.
Because I, also, am different from everyone around me.
But I don't know how to live.
I am lost.

Resentment comes.
It isn't fair.
Because I don't have a socio-political place to belong.
There is no wolfpack for me, no tribe.
I'm just me.
Alone.
Strange, stunned, and unable to explain.

And then I make the impossible decision.
I decide I'm not going to do it.
I'm just not.

A LUCKY BREATH

I'm not going to try to color inside the lines anymore.
For the benefit of whom should I do it?
The lesbian couples aren't doing it, and I'm not doing it either.
I don't have to.
I don't have to be anything.
I don't have to do anything.
Nobody has to understand me or approve of my life.
I don't owe anything to anyone.
I don't have to meet anyone's expectations—not even those of my previous selves.
I can just be me and that's good enough.
And I am leaving.
I am leaving this cold city and going home.
I am going where the air doesn't hurt to breathe.

The day I realized Enrique could drink until he hurt someone, it was himself that he'd injured. I wasn't even there.

The month before we got married, I flew back to Pennsylvania to spend Christmas with my family. In the 18 months that I'd lived in Costa Rica, this was my first visit home. I only had money for one ticket and after that was gone there would be no more, so I was saving it in case of an emergency. Eventually, being as I showed no present intention of moving north, my parents offered to fly me home for the holidays.

Before I left Santa Cruz, I gave Enrique the number to the phone in my parents' home and careful instructions on how to place international collect calls from a public phone. I asked him to please call me sometimes.

In my letters, I'd told my parents about my boyfriend Enrique. This was their worst nightmare and I knew it. They'd feared that I might fall in love with someone of a different religion, a different language, a different culture, and never come home. I dreaded telling them about him, but I did it. I had to. They demonstrated polite interest when I talked about Enrique, but didn't ask many questions. I promised myself I wouldn't leave without telling them about the wedding. I didn't mention that we lived together, now. Having to break the news that I was going to have a Costa Rican husband was bad enough, never mind having to tell them I was also signed up to go to hell.

I had a marvelous time there in the farmhouse full of sisters and brothers-in-law. A fire burned day and night in the fireplace, snow fell outside, and I gobbled down dozens of foods I'd practically forgotten about and that upset my stomach after 18 months of rice and beans.

Half way through my visit, Enrique called from the payphone near our house. He told me he'd had a bicycle accident on the way home from work, and that he'd broken his front teeth. I was horrified. He promised me he was alright other than the teeth, and that the car that caused him to lose control hadn't hit him. He said the bike was ok—he'd gotten it fixed. I died a thousand deaths inside, imagining him flying through the air. My parents prayed for his safety when they said grace over dinner.

The day before I left, I told my parents Enrique and I were going to get married. In a week or two. They said they knew it was no use to argue, so we didn't. Their main concern was about religion. They asked me worriedly whether we would raise our children to be Catholic or Protestant. I told them I didn't know. They wept at the airport when we said goodbye, something they had ever done before. Our family isn't one to cry in airports or display negative emotions. We laugh when we're having fun, but we swallow our anger and keep our tears to ourselves. There was nothing I could say, no type of comfort I could offer my parents as I stood awkwardly beside my suitcases. I explained to them that we would sign papers with a lawyer, have a small meal, and that would be all. It wasn't going to be something they needed to plan a trip to Costa Rica for. I was relieved that they didn't try.

The first thing I did when I got back home was to take Enrique to the dentist and pay to fix his teeth. A broken piece of root that remained in his gum was causing a painful infection and needed to come out immediately. Then a post had to be set for a crown, and the other front tooth needed to be ground down and capped as well. Soon, he was smiling normally again.

I learned the truth months later. There was no bicycle accident. Enrique got blasted drunk and out of hand at the cantina in Los Ríos one Sunday afternoon. He drank so much that he became ornery, then aggressive. He started a fight with some of the other men, kicking, punching, and shouting at them for no apparent reason. The bartender threw him out and told him not to come back, but Enrique was out of his mind. No sooner was he outside the bar, than he turned around and came back in. He shouted and pushed people. Someone called the police.

Enrique never even got on the bike he said he wrecked. That explains why, even after an accident bad enough to break his teeth, the bike looked perfectly fine. The owner of the cantina brought the bicycle inside where it would be safe after the police came and Enrique took off staggering up the road. He had no recollection of the police. Nor walking away from the cantina. He knew he fell into a ditch and slept there until morning because that's where he woke up the next day with no money, no shoes, and broken front teeth. Then he got up and walked the 12 kilometers back to Santa Cruz with no idea what had happened.

This wasn't Enrique's first drinking binge, but it was the first one that affected me. I didn't know what to do when I found out about it. Becoming angry seemed like a waste of energy—by the time I got back from my trip, he was sober, sorry, and ashamed. I decided that if I had been there with him, where I belonged, this wouldn't have happened. It wasn't that I blamed myself; I blamed the situation. Enrique wasn't really like that. I spread the guilt around far enough that it became thin and light.

In the morning, I call Delta Airlines.
The travel agent in San Jose could sell me a round trip ticket cheaper than a one-way, so I actually have a flight back.
I hadn't planned to use it, but I have a new plan.
I change the date.
In two weeks I'm going home.
I'm not going to grad school.
I'm not going to get a job "helping" "the poor" or being a hamburger.
I take my clothes back to the store for a refund.

Michelle is stricken.
I know she is frightened for me, but I'm going to be okay.
She is afraid I will go back to Enrique like I did before.
I know I won't.
My parents are horrified.
They try to spare me their fear and disappointment, but of course I perceive it.
I'm not going back to Enrique.
I'm going back to me.

I'm hungry.
I stop crying and start eating again.
I'm starving.
Costa Rica is a small country, but it's not so small that I can't find a place to live besides in Los Ríos with Enrique.
I need to face him.
I need to see the children.
I need to get a divorce, and go on living.
No more being cold.

No more useless, chilly sunshine.
David calls me collect on the phone.

I tell him I'm coming home.
He says I can live with him in Puntarenas.
He says he knew I would come back to him.
I don't want to live with David in Puntarenas.
I don't want to live with Enrique in Los Ríos.
I want to live in San José far away from everyone.
I want to get a divorce.
I want to start a new life.
But all of it is so far away, and I'm so happy to hear David's warm voice.
I miss him.
I miss being loved.
I tell him when I will arrive, and he says he'll meet me at the airport.
That sounds nice so I say alright.

A LUCKY BREATH

❧

I could have acknowledged things were not what I thought they were when I heard about Sandrita, but I decided to believe Enrique instead. I wanted so much for the rumors to be false that I blamed the baby on Angel and refused to think about the rest. Enrique and I had a sweet simple life in Santa Cruz. We were planning our little January wedding. I would apply for residence after we were married, and never have to leave Costa Rica or Enrique. I wanted these things more than anything, including the truth.

When Enrique came home from work that day, he said that he had to talk to me, but he wouldn't look at my eyes. He was obviously miserable. He said he had to tell me something that would make me so angry I might leave him. I felt ill. He wasn't joking. He laid on the bed on his back and looked at the ceiling. I laid beside him on my belly staring at him, waiting. I tried to touch him but he wouldn't let me. Sandrita, he finally told me, is pregnant. And Sandrita is saying that the baby is his.

My hands went numb. Sandrita was the teenage girl who cleans Los Ríos houses for pennies, and helped María when she baked bread. She was the oldest daughter of Juana, the washer woman.

I asked him if he had been with her.

He said "yes but" so quickly it sounded like one word. "Yes but" only once or twice. Before he was with me. And besides, he said, daring to look at me because this was supposed to matter, Angel had been with her much more. And Enrique was sure that the baby was Angel's. He was sure she was lying when she said it wasn't—lying because she imagined that since Enrique was with me, he had lots of money that she could get for herself and the baby.

It was November. I counted backwards. We rented this house in Santa Cruz together three months ago in August. Four months ago, in July, we first started hatching plans to get married. Six months ago, in May, Enrique came to Playa Celeste with me hoping to find work and planning to live with me. Our first night together was in March, eight months ago. Unless Sandrita was already overdue, which she wasn't, we were together. We were definitely together. In February when I'd begun my job in Playa Celeste in the real estate office, I missed him viscerally all week long. I lived for the weekends when I could go home to Los Ríos and we would go dancing. He said he loved me. I believed him. It hadn't occurred to me to be suspicious or jealous. In my mind, we were together since the first kiss in the deserted bleachers one mid-January dawn 11 months ago. But it didn't matter. Regardles where you start counting from, there is no possible way we weren't together.

Enrique promised me he wasn't cheating on me with Sandrita. Besides, it only happened once or twice. A long time ago. That's all he would say. He begged me not to leave him. He promised me he wanted only me. He pleaded with me to believe him that the baby wasn't his. And if it was—if he was that unlucky—what was he supposed to do about it now?

And what was I supposed to do? Leave him now because we had different ideas about when we became "together?" Lose my chance at a resident status, a life, a home, a family?

I chose to accept Enrique's explanations. The damage, now, was done no matter who'd done it. I could either forgive him for cheating and lying to me while I was away in Playa Celeste dreaming of him, or I could throw everything away. Call off the wedding, find a new place to live, figure out another way to apply for residency, and start over from zero. I decided that the baby was Angel's. And even if Enrique had been with Sandrita, he wasn't now. I didn't let myself think about it. I didn't admit to myself that on those weekends he was lying to me. But I did remember the Monday morning I saw him sitting beside Sandrita in the plaza when the *bus that was taking me away to work rounded the corner, and the strange little smiles on their faces when I waved.*

I never told anyone about baby Melani. She was born an angry little girl who screamed and bit and would not go to school. She lied from the moment she could speak and stole from the moment she could make a fist. To this day nobody knows which brother is her daddy, but she looks just like her sisters and cousins, whichever may be which.

It was a clear warning. It was my chance to save myself, but I wasn't interested.

※

I put everything I own back into the suitcases and Michelle drives me to the airport.
David will meet my flight.
He has begged me to go to Puntarenas with him, so I agree.
For a few days.
Why not?
Then I will go back to San José, find an apartment, and get a job.
An apartment and a job will be easy for me to find in the capital.
When I'm ready, I will call Enrique and meet him face to face.
I have to.
I'm not the kind of girl who runs away.

My sense of relief is tremendous.
Now I am telling the truth, and the truth is that I don't know anything.
I don't know where I'm going.
I don't know what I'm going to do.
I don't know how I will live my life.
I don't know if I'm making a terrible mistake by going back to Costa Rica, or if I made a terrible mistake when I left.
I don't know if I've ever done anything that hasn't been a terrible mistake.
I don't care.
I'm not sorry.
I'm done trying to be good.
I'm done trying to do everything right.
I'm done trying to be careful, safe, and reasonable.
The only thing that matters to me is that in a few hours when I get off the plane, I will be in Costa Rica.

A LUCKY BREATH

In Costa Rica, I know things.

I know bus schedules, radio stations, phone numbers, what brand of shampoo to buy, and whether or not it will rain.

In the United States, I know nothing.

I only know I don't want to be cold, help "the poor", or be a hamburger.

We decided to get married. Enrique didn't drop to one knee and produce a ring or anything, he just told me one day that he wanted to marry me and left me to ponder it speechlessly for a while. At first, I was mortified by the idea. It seemed like it couldn't possibly work. But as I considered my options, I realized that in the end I was going to either feed this relationship and see what it grew into, or starve it. When someone asks to marry you, you can't say "sort of." It's all or none. I picked all. We started saving money and the process of obtaining documents.

Two months later, we rented a house in Santa Cruz. This solved all of our problems except the fact that we had nothing. No table, no chairs, no refrigerator, no stove, no couch, no coffee mugs—nothing. I brought my bed and mattress from Playa Celeste. That is where we ate, slept, and lounged, listening to the radio. I had a set of wooden shelves we stacked our clothes on. Enrique borrowed a little square table from the pottery workshop so we had a place to set the electric frying pan and rice maker that I bought. We had our bicycles. I bought plates, cups, a broom, and a fan. Now, instead of living in three places, I could live in one. No more living five days a week in Playa Celeste then spending weekends in Los Ríos shuffling between where I lived at Mateo and Norma's house, and Enrique's workshop nest. I was on cloud nine.

Having no money carried no stigma. There was no shame in it, nor did anyone try to avoid it. For us and everyone like us—which was everyone—having no money was a given. It is a lifestyle we knew and accepted.

Each morning at five o'clock I heated water in the electric frying pan and poured it through a sock-shaped cloth bag with coffee grounds the way coffee has been brewed for centuries. Then I rinsed the pan and cooked our gallo pinto in it. I sat crosswise on the bar of my bicycle while Enrique pedaled, delivering me to the bus stop at 7 AM. Then he kissed me goodbye and turned to ride the 12 kilometers to Los Ríos to the pottery workshop. I took the bus as close to Playa Celeste as I could, then hitchhiked the rest of the way.

In the evenings after work, I bought each day's perishables at the pulperia—just enough for a meal or two, because we could not dream of buying a refrigerator. I made our dinner of rice and beans with perhaps a slice of fresh cheese or fried eggs, sometimes canned tuna, or something special like fried pieces of a giant hot dog called a salchicón. We accompanied this with boiled green or ripe platanos and scalding black coffee. Stewed chicken or beef were for occasions like payday. We ate early, as soon as both of us were home and the food was ready. We were ridiculously happy, then. We got a dog.

At night after dinner, before we married and had enough money to buy the little TV, I washed the dishes and we turned off the lights. It was barely 7 o'clock, but there was nothing else to do. We lay on our bed in the dark in front of the fan listening to the radio. There was nothing else we wanted to do, nowhere else we wanted to go, no one else we would have rather been with than with each other lying on that bed. Commenting on the songs. Laughing at commercials. Guessing what song would come next and never once being right. Telling stories. Listing to each other. Everything was easy and simple. Nothing was confusing, difficult, or painful. We had exactly what we needed each day—nothing more and nothing less.

We fell asleep early and woke before the alarm, anxious. I feigned sleep, pretending I didn't know when Enrique would reach for me, pretending to be surprised to find him awake and ready. He loved that—my pretend confusion, my weak resistance. It was an easy game we never tired of playing.

On Saturdays, Enrique rode to work in Los Ríos and I stayed

home. I washed our clothes and bedding by hand in the cement sink on the back porch and hung it all to dry in the sun. Towels, sheets, underwear, stained socks to be scrubbed but not stretched, clay-crusted work clothes, jeans, and button-down shirts from the night we went dancing all went into the sink, then onto the line to dry. When I finished, I was spent, drenched in suds and sweat, knuckles raw, wrists limp, back splitting, dizzy with exhaustion and the kind of relief that comes from clean clothes and a task completed.

The neighbor woman, washing in the sink on the back porch next door, told me all about her daughters and asked when we would have children. I told her soon. Hopefully, soon. Enrique said a house without children is empty, and I understood he wanted me to be pregnant. I couldn't imagine how we would survive if I stayed home to raise children, but "soon" seemed like the right answer. Other people did it, so we would figure it out, too.

Part V: Puntarenas

David is waiting for me at the airport.
I am so happy to be home, so happy that the cold blur of sadness and confusion in Atlanta is over.
I clutch David in a delighted embrace.
He kisses me, bubbling with joy.
He says he knew I would come back to marry him.
He says he was sure I would
His eyes are moist with tears.
A touch of nausea creeps into my stomach.
At no time have I said this or anything like it.
He hasn't understood because he refuses to.
I haven't come back to marry him.
I haven't come back to marry anyone.
I have come to get a divorce.
I have come to start over on my own.

David presses that we must go to Puntarenas.
His uncles and cousins are waiting to meet me.
He has told them all about me.

We can take jobs there, he assures me, rent a house, and we will be very happy.
It's all wrong, but I cannot find the words to make him stop.
He is so heartbreakingly joyful.
And I have nowhere I need to go.
No one is expecting me anywhere.
I have told no one about my return.
The goodbyes I said when I left were permanent.
I am starting over from scratch.
I'm not going back to Enrique or to Los Ríos no matter what anyone thinks or fears I might do.
I am floating in the air.
A taxi takes David and me from the airport to the Puntarenas bus terminal.
It's alright, I think.
Why not?
Just for a day or two.
I should be strong and say I don't want to go, but I am tired.
I will worry about tomorrow when it gets here, break David's heart another day.

On the afternoon of the same day that Michelle drops me at the Atlanta airport with my suitcases, I board a bus with David to Puntarenas.

A LUCKY BREATH

※

Carina María doesn't remember a time when she didn't know me. In her memory, I am always there. She was two years old the first time she fell asleep in my arms.

She wore an olive-green dress with a little pink flower on the afternoon Enrique brought her to the pottery workshop that had become his new home. He missed waking up every morning to the kids, especially little Carina. On a lazy Sunday afternoon, he went to fetch her from her mama's house for a few hours.

I wanted the children to like me. I feared their resentment and hoped for their love. The school-aged boys were easy to engage, but little Carina María was mutely skeptical. She stared at me with the suspicious eyes of a toddler who has heard what people say, and understands.

Enrique rode away from the pottery workshop on his bicycle and returned with Carina in one arm. And there we were, the three of us, working out our new family. She eyed me from the safety of her daddy's embrace. I tried to make her laugh.

A neighbor wandered by looking for Enrique, asking him for help to fix something at the house. Enrique never said no to a friend. He told me he'd be right back and got up to go. I wanted to tell him not to leave me with Carina. Not yet. What will I do with her? We were two complete strangers. But words failed me, and in a moment, he was gone. Then it was just little Carina María and me looking at each other, trying to decide what happens next. I thought she might cry, but at two she was already brave.

Pottery shops are full of things children aren't allowed to touch, so I pulled the tube of lipstick out of my pocket. We played hide and seek with it in the cardboard boxes piled in the corner. Carina liked that game. She toddled around the boxes with staccato steps and stopped staring at me as if I were an intruder. She laughed and chattered things to me that I couldn't understand.

Eventually, she tired. She held her little hands up to me when I reached down to pick her up. The afternoon heat was heavy, and so much heavier with a toddler pressed to my chest. I sat on the front steps of the workshop rocking little Carina María who slumped into sleep in my arms.

That's now Enrique found us when he returned—Carina and me having made our peace. He smiled.

A LUCKY BREATH

❦

The bus spits us out in Puntarenas, a humid, dirty port city.
The air reeks of boiling asphalt, dog shit, and fish from the tuna packing plants.
In Puntarenas it is impossible to breathe.
The only other foreigners here are Nicaraguans.
This town is of little interest to tourists or students of culture.
Only people poor enough to have to pack fish live here.
David has been here during the six weeks I shivered in Atlanta.
He hasn't gotten a job.
I realize that he hasn't tried.
He was waiting.
For me to come back.
At least, in Atlanta, I tried.

David takes me to the uncle's house where he lives.
The house sets in a row of identical concrete boxes with a kitchen/living area, a bathroom, two bedrooms, and a porch.
Behind the house is a small patio that serves as a laundry, a playground for the children, and a bathroom for the dogs.
Counting David and me, fifteen people live in the house: the uncle, the aunt, the uncle's brother, several cousins and their spouses, and the grandchildren.
There are half-sisters and half-brothers.
No one who can be called family will be without a roof and a plate of rice and beans.
This now includes me.
This is the meaning of "family," here.
In my three suitcases I have more possessions than the other 14 of them put together.
They receive us warmly, curiously, generously.

Now that the American wife has arrived, things are going to change for everyone, especially for David.
Scarcity is over.
No one says this directly.
It is woven into the fabric of our interactions.

David's bed is a roll of foam.
At night, he opens it on the living room floor by the wall.
The bedrooms are full to bursting with human bodies.
Half of the porch has been turned into a bedroom, and it is full.
The couch is a bed.
There are beds in the kitchen.
I pull sheets out of my suitcase and share the foam with David.
The first night, I am exhausted, numb, and grateful.
I am grateful for the warm air that wraps me again in its forgiving embrace.
I am grateful to be closing my eyes where I can hear crickets singing to the moon, the neighbor's radio, uncles laughing on the porch.
I am grateful for the smiles of a family that has no questions, no agenda, no judgement.

Enrique was furious at Inez for attacking me. He took his clothes, the mattress from his bed, and his mosquito net, and moved out of the house. These things he placed in a corner on the floor of the new pottery workshop that he, Mateo, and a group of friends inaugurated a few months before. He would save money to buy plywood and nails to partition off the corner. In the mornings and evenings, he rode his bicycle across town to his parents' house for showers and meals, then returned to the shop where he worked and slept.

This unmarried Enrique, and he was all mine. Weekends home from Playa Celeste became completely different. I needed to eat, shower, and wash my clothes at Mateo and Norma's house, but there was no need for Enrique and me to lie about our relationship anymore. At night, we slept under the mosquito net while the open-mouthed pottery watched over us. He took me with him to Martín and María's house where they received me as part of the family. We rode our bicycles to the dances, and we didn't care who saw us. Every day was the best day of my life.

Norma was livid. She stormed around the house like a thundercloud. She stopped talking to me. She wouldn't even look at me. If I addressed her, she answered coldly. All the warmth of our Sunday afternoons drinking hot coffee and giggling at gossip was gone. No more windy mornings cooking gallo pinto together over the fire. No more soap operas on TV or naps on her bed in front of the fan. I understood the injurious meanings of each of her tirades of silence. Her fury broke my heart.

She knew she couldn't tell me what to do. She knew she couldn't throw me out of the house for being with Enrique even though she wanted to. I was Mateo's friend too, and Mateo didn't care what

I did. Mateo shrugged his shoulders and told me to be careful of Enrique's temper, but he couldn't help being happy for us. I wasn't worried about Enrique's temper. Enrique loved me. His temper was a problem for other people.

I considered leaving Mateo and Norma's house, but I couldn't think of anywhere else to go. In the meantime, I tried to be unobtrusive and not cause any more problems than I already had.

I loved Norma. I wished she could be happy for me like Mateo was. For a time, we had seemed so the same, and suddenly we were so opposite. I hoped that with time, she might come around and be my friend again.

But Norma loved order, cleanliness, and rules. Norma, with her machete for kindling, her giant Bible, her curly hair, her contagious laugh, her withering frown, and her prestiños frying. Norma was studying to be a teacher. She became a principal. She could do anything she set her mind to, including eradicate evil from her home.

She made me choose, and I chose Enrique.

A LUCKY BREATH

The next day when I wake up in Puntarenas, I am less exhausted, less numb, and less grateful.
There are too many of us in this house.
I have got to get out.
David and I walk a few blocks to a public telephone.
I call my mother and lie to her.
I tell her I am in San José with Rebeca and her family, that I'm doing fine, and that I'll be looking for work in a day or two.
I don't tell her I am in a dirty fish city in a house with 14 Nicaraguans who think I am the new member of their family.
I try to sound happy and relieved.
I tell David I need to buy a newspaper.
I say I want to look for jobs and apartments in San José.
David says a neighbor down the street has a house we can rent.
I say I want to live in San José.
He says ok, we can live in San José.
I don't say we.
David says we.
I should correct him, but I don't.
I don't know how.
On the way home, we buy food: rice, tuna, coffee, and sugar.
It isn't fair for them to house us and feed us as well.
Of course, we buy more than we need so that we can share.
Sharing is the rule.
It's a good rule, and I agree with it.
But I know how it works, now.
I can see that I must find a way to leave Puntarenas quickly, even if it isn't graceful.
I am not going to do for David's family in Puntarenas what I did for David's family in Nicaragua.
Absolutely not.

At night, I can't sleep.
The foam is thin, and the floor is hard.
When I go to bed it is too hot and when I wake later, the dampness feels cold.
There are cockroaches in the house.
Big cockroaches.
I imagine them crawling across the floor onto the dirty foam.
I float above my body and see myself lying on the floor in Puntarenas, the ugliest place in this beautiful country, with no hope of finding my life until I leave.
I have to get out of here.
I have to be alone.
I cannot think in this house.
I cannot sleep.
I cannot breathe.
I cannot be absorbed into this family or this life because this is not why I got back on the plane.
My life in Los Ríos, in spite of everything that was wrong, was a thousand times better than this.
In Los Ríos, I had a house and a family.
I don't even love this man.
He isn't my husband.
I have a husband.
My husband is not David.
These children are not my children.
My children wonder every day where I am and why I left them.
I am so near them now.
They would race into my arms if they saw me.
These are the wrong children.

Things disappear from my suitcases when we are not home.
A pair of flip-flops.
A new sports bra.
The extra tube of toothpaste.

Of course Enrique lied to Inez about where he had been when he came back home after his failed attempt to run away with me. Of course she knew the truth perfectly well. At first she refused to let him back in the house. She slammed the door and told him to leave. But the children cried and little Carina screamed, "Mi papi! Mi papi!" until she opened the door.

Shortly after that, she waited for us late one night behind the giant gallinazo tree beside the road and surprised us on our way home from a dance. Enrique and I had ridden our bicycles separately to San Vicente, five kilometers up the road, where a live band played loud cheerful music into the warm night. Everyone danced and drank beer and Coca-Cola poured into cups full of ice. I'd anticipated this all week, hoping that the weather would hold, that Enrique would meet me at the dance, that everything would work out the way it had.

We'd drank a lot of beer, and we wanted to make the journey home under the merciful cover of night take as long as possible, so we walked beside our bicycles instead of riding them.

Enrique would have accompanied me home, back to the front door of Mateo and Norma's house like a gentleman. He was going to kiss me in the shadows, even though he wasn't supposed to, and he was going to ride his bike back to his house. And go to sleep. We were almost there. Then as we passed the towering gallinazo in front of María's house, Inez jumped out at us from behind the trunk. She shouted at us and came for me. I put my hands up to protect my face. Her curled fist came down with a furious rap on my collar bone.

Enrique shouted, dropped his bicycle in the dust, and lunged at her. As they scuffled and screamed into the peaceful midnight of crickets, I mounted my bike and rode away in heart-pounding horror. She attacked me. Not him. Me.

I pedaled away without looking back. The screaming behind me got louder. I hoped they weren't hitting each other. I hoped this wasn't my fault. I knew it was. I wondered if Enrique would ever speak to me again. I wondered if Inez would attack me in broad daylight. At the pulperia. On the street. At the bus stop.

I was getting further away, but the screaming became louder, not quieter. I slunk into Mateo and Norma's dark house and slipped gratefully inside with my bicycle. Except for a tender point on my collar bone, the assault had been verbal.

Los Ríos is small. I turned on the fan and lie petrified on my little bed listening to Enrique's entire family scream at each other. Doors and windows slammed. The children were crying. The brothers, the parents—everyone was awake in the night shouting and slamming and screaming—first guttural, then shrill. I lay wide-eyed on my bed wondering, my God what have I done?

You did this, I told myself. You did this.

It sounded like the end of the world unfolding just across the pasture, and I knew that in the morning everyone in Los Ríos would have heard the whole story. Los Ríos is too small for secrets. Its rumors are always true.

I felt sorry, that night. I felt sorry for Inez. I felt sorry for the children I could hear crying. I felt sorry for María. I heard her shouting his name while he roared. I felt sorry I had ever spoken to Enrique. What is wrong with me? Why am I doing this? I hated myself. I should have left Los Ríos months ago in September, I thought. That was when I stopped seeing The Boy—the one I'd come back to Los Ríos for, the one who'd promised he'd love me forever but didn't. Or maybe he did. But in my absence, he'd acquired a pubescent girlfriend. I didn't mind about her. I'd had boyfriends too while I finished college and worked out how to come back here. But I left them for him, and he did not leave her for me. I should have swallowed my pride and gone home, not gotten involved with Enrique. It was the closing of a door, the agonizing end of a story I *thought would be endless. I should have packed my bags and taken a bus to somewhere else the next day. But I didn't. The night Inez attacked me, I wished I had. I wished I had never seen Enrique, that he had stayed in the banana plantations of Guapiles forever. I wished I'd had the sense to ignore his timid smiles.*

The next morning, Mateo went to Enrique's house and brought back the rest of the story. In the scuffle between Enrique and Inez, María intervened. Enrique shoved her and she fell. Angel leapt on Enrique and Enrique, drunk and furious, grabbed him by the throat and shook. Neighbors ran from their homes to keep Martín from killing Enrique with his bare hands after Enrique injured Inez, María, and Angel.

For weeks afterward, Angel wore a padded collar to brace his injured neck. Years passed before Martín and Enrique spoke to each other again, and before brothers were willing to be in the same room together. The family was fragmented.

I promised myself it wasn't my fault. Everything that happened after Inez's fist thumped my collar bone was not up to me. But I knew it was my fault it ever started.

After that, there were no more secrets.

Zimmerman

※

I am even more lost in Puntarenas than I was in Atlanta.
I am much more lost than the day I drove away from Enrique in the little truck.
I don't want this.
How did I end up here?
Everything about this is wrong.
But I can't summon the lucidity to decide what to do.
I can't think.
So I make a list.
I write all my problems on a paper.
It's a long list.
I order them from the biggest to the smallest.
I must get out of the house in Puntarenas.
That's the biggest problem.
To do that, I need to find an apartment in San José.
The apartment must be the first thing to do.
And I need a job.
But the job is the second thing on the list, not the first.
After I have an apartment, I can worry about the job.
I must contact Enrique, but that can wait too.
I don't know what to do about David, so I don't do anything.
I buy a newspaper.
I go to the public telephone down the street and call the numbers for apartments I can afford.
David comes with me and listens to me talking.
I make appointments to see the apartments tomorrow.
We go back to the house and I pack an overnight bag.
David packs a bag too.
In the morning, he gets on the bus with me and goes to San José.

I find an apartment I can afford.
It is a terribly sad place, but not the most terrible or the saddest we see that day.
I pay the deposit and the first month's rent.
This apartment is one of six located in the yard behind a building supply company.
My apartment is on the second floor.
That makes me feel safe.
A wooden stairway leads from the ground to a small porch and the door.
Inside, the small apartment is dark.
The tiny kitchen, consisting of a tiny plastic sink with faucet, is in one corner of the living area.
Beside the kitchen, there is a bathroom with an icy shower.
There is a bedroom that has a small closet and the apartment's only window overlooking tin roofs.
This is good enough.
It's what I can afford.
The supply company's gate will keep me safe.
I sleep with David in a cheap hotel and we go back to Puntarenas the next day.
I need to get my things.
I spend one last night in the house with too many people, and I get back on the bus with my cargo of suitcases.
David comes with me.
He doesn't ask me what I want.
He assumes.
We don't talk about it.
I have no words.
I just go and he just goes with me.
He believes I am going to marry him.
Later, when I feel better.
I don't believe anything.
We move into the dark apartment in San José.

I don't know how to make him go away.
I try to think about it, but I can't think.

Now, the biggest problems are solved.
I am out of Puntarenas.
I have an apartment.
Next, I have to go shopping, because the apartment has nothing in it.
I buy the cheapest full-size mattress I can find – a piece of foam covered with cloth, for $35.
I buy a shower curtain and two trash cans, one for the bathroom and one for the kitchen.
I buy a four-burner stove top.
Two burners are electric, and two can connect to a propane tank.
I have options.
I don't have options now because I can't afford the propane tank, but someday I will.
After I find a job.
I buy two metal pots—one for rice and one for beans—a frying pan for eggs, and a small tin kettle for making coffee.
I buy two plates, two bowls, two mugs, two spoons, two forks, and two knives.
I buy a broom, a mop, a toilet brush, and a blue bucket.
David and I take these things home to the apartment in the barrio called San Francisco de Dos Ríos.
I feel like a queen.
I have a bed.
My very own bed.
Even in Atlanta, in the luxury of Michelle's house, my bed did not belong to me.
This one is mine.
A roof and a bed.

For months, we saw each other secretly. We couldn't go on actual dates or have hotel rendezvous because there is no place to go in Los Ríos. The best we could do was to steal out of dances and then back in, or ride our bicycles under the cover of night to the river, to the woods, to the plaza of the next town. We made love in the earth's secret places like our ancestors—in the meadow by the corral, in a mountain stream, nestled between the clawing roots of giant trees. Night was the perfect blanket. Small towns are a bad place for big secrets. Rumors circulated. We denied them.

Then we decided that Enrique would run away with me, like eloping, but without the wedding ceremony. It was the same thing in our world. He said he wanted out of the house where he lived with the furious mother of his children. He said that relationship was over and had been for a long time, that she didn't love him and he didn't love her. He used to, he said, but not anymore. He said he only stayed there with her because he didn't have anywhere else to go. I believed him.

Enrique and I decided he would come to live with me in Playa Celeste. A lot of construction was going on, and certainly we would find work for him. He would earn more money working at the coast than in the pottery shop in Los Ríos, and could better support the children. We wanted to be together. Both of us were done caring how difficult it would be, what people would think, or what people would say. I'd moved to the house of an Italian couple where I had my own room and use of the home's common areas. It was much more than the tiny room above the deli. The Italian couple did not smile when I told them my Costa Rican boyfriend was coming to live with me. They didn't say no or throw me out, but they were obviously displeased. They needed my money, so they frowned, but nodded.

On a cloudy May morning, we left Los Ríos on different buses. What we'd done wouldn't be a secret for long, but at least Enrique would be able to leave his house without a fight. I always took a bus out of town on Monday mornings, so there was nothing unusual about me waiting by the road with my backpack. It would be harder for Enrique. The idea of packing his things and walking out of the house caused him alternating moments of relief and agony. He didn't want to walk away from his little ones. He knew Carina would cry.

We'd decided to meet an hour down the road in Belen. It was raining in Belen when I arrived—the kind of steamy tropical rain where sun periodically burns through clouds while water keeps falling. I got off the bus and sat on the bench to wait. Buses stopped, unloaded, took on new passengers, and left. People looked perplexedly at me, a foreigner with a big pack watching buses come and go but never getting on one. I was waiting for the one that would open its door and release my lover—the man I swore I would do anything for. I had tried so hard not to fall in love with him, and I had failed completely. Every single breath I took without him near me was excruciating. I would sit there all day if I had to. I would sit there all night. The interminable weeks without him in Playa Celeste were over now, and a new life was beginning right then—I could feel it. I knew if he just summoned the nerve to walk out the door, everything would be alright. He had to do that part alone. All the rest, we would do together, starting today. I waited a long time.

A lightning bolt of electricity shot through me when Enrique's curly head appeared in the line of passengers stepping down from the bus into the bright rain. He carried a giant green backpack that contained everything he owned. And he was wearing his cowboy boots. That's how I knew he was serious: he wore the boots. I felt that the whole world ended and was reborn at that moment. It would never be the same.

The world was, in fact, never the same, but Enrique didn't stay with me in Playa Celeste. He couldn't do it. He didn't even make it to the weekend. In a matter of days, he carried his green pack back home to the house with the angry Inez and delighted children.

The job search didn't go well, or not the way Enrique envisioned. It went like job searches go—unpleasant, discouraging, and interspersed with too much free time. He said Playa Celeste was alright as a place to visit, but not a place to live. Not for him. Things were too expensive. There were too many languages and not enough Spanish. The Italian couple I lived with eyed him suspiciously, as if all brown-skinned men were criminals. He said he missed the kids. He worried about little Carina María.

I was crushed, but there was no use arguing. He was right. Playa Celeste was an easy place for me, but it was not an easy place for Enrique. I cried after he left, took a few deep breaths, and let it go. We loved each other and we'd think of another way to work it out.

Part VI:
San Francisco de Dos Ríos

David never asks me if I want him to live with me.
I never tell him I don't.
He assumes I don't want to be alone the way he doesn't want to be alone.
He assures me that he's going to get a job right away.
He promises he will give me all his money so that we can buy nice furniture, get married, and have babies.
I tell him I can't think about that.
He won't listen.
My attempts to say no are weak, and he refuses to accept them.
In his mind, there is no room for doubt.
One day, he believes, I will go out and get a divorce the way I went out and got the mattress we sleep on.
The way I announced I was coming back from Atlanta.
The way I have always done everything.
He is certain.

I have no friends other than David.
I have no one else to talk to.

Most of the time I don't mind him.
He knows me.
He loves me.
I wish in my heart that he would decide to go away, but I don't have the strength to say it to him.
I am completely numb.
I have no idea what is going to happen—not tomorrow, not next week, not next year.
I can't even think about it.
I can only think about one thing at a time.
I can only think that now, since I have found an apartment, I need to find a job.

Every morning, I buy a newspaper, and David and I look for jobs.
We save 20 colon coins to use in the public phone across the street.
I think I might like an office job.
I could teach English, but I don't want to.
I can't be a teacher right now.
I need an easy job where I don't have to think much.
A boring job would be perfect—one I can do without concentrating—because I can't concentrate.
My mind refuses to focus on anything.
And I need a flexible schedule, because I am going to have to go to Los Ríos.
I am going to have to get a divorce, and I just might miss a few days of work.
I circle the jobs that are near the center of San José because I like the idea of working downtown.
I circle jobs that require English, offer good pay, and advertise flexible hours.
The resume and references I prepared in Atlanta should be

more than enough to get me any job I want, here.
I am overqualified for everything that interests me.
David reads the ads and smokes cigarettes.
He has a work permit for Costa Rica, but no resume and no references.
No work experience except farming and pottery.
I schedule interviews.

I wear my best clothes and go downtown.
The interviews are all at something called "sports books."
I've never heard of a "sports book."
At the first interview, I learn that sports books are North American gambling companies.
Since gambling on sports events is illegal in the United States, companies set up their offices in other countries.
They receive bets over the phone.
Obviously, fluent English is required.
I've never bet on anything in my life, and I've never cared about sports.
It's the perfect job for me.
All I have to do is answer the phone and enter numbers into a computer.
I don't have to think or care about anything.

The first company I visit is very formal.
The office is somber and dim.
They ask me why I want this job if I don't know anything about betting or sports.
They offer me good money because of my English, but the schedule is stone.
They say I can start on Monday if I want.
I say I will let them know what I decide.
The second interview is completely disorganized.

A LUCKY BREATH

The company is still moving into their office on the second story of a building by a park.
Lots of windows that look out over trees.
Telephone parts spill from boxes and only half of the computer monitors have arrived.
The man who interviews me looks younger than I am.
The partners are there plugging in telephones and tripping over chairs.
They look like athletic boys who never talked to me in college.
They offer me less money, but they say they will be as flexible as I want.
They tell me I can start any time.
I say, "Monday."

Now that I make four dollars an hour, I'm not poor anymore.
It's an excellent wage, and I love my job.
I love going to work.
I love getting dressed and riding the bus.
I love looking out the window of the bus, watching the city zoom by this rolling room full of strangers.
I love being at work.
I have a desk, a chair, and a computer.
I have to learn a lot of number codes, but it's an easy job.
When my phone rings, I have an anonymous conversation with somebody who wants to bet money on a sports game.
That's all.
I don't need to care about anything.
I don't even have to watch the game.
I can think about whatever I want.
I can read books when the afternoon is slow.
Sometimes my coworkers and I order food to be delivered.
I can drink coffee.
I can look out the window.

The TV is on all the time.
I stare at it, forgetting everything except the little blobs of color moving around.
The other employees are all Costa Ricans, and all younger than I am.
The girls are nice to me.
They ask me if I have a boyfriend.
I say no.
I tell them I'm separated from my husband.
I don't tell them about David.
They can't find out.
David isn't my boyfriend.
He lives with me because I had an affair with him, and now I don't know how to throw him out.
It's all wrong.
That much, I am well aware of.
The fun-loving owners of the sports book take everyone out for drinks on Tuesday nights, and I never go.
I can't.
I would have to take David, and I am not taking David.
No one must know about him.
I am ashamed.

A LUCKY BREATH

∽∂

Soon after I started working Playa Celeste, Enrique came to see me. For the first time ever, no one was watching over us. No nosey neighbors. No glowering Inez. No furious Norma.

Enrique told Inez that he was going off to the mountains with one of his cousins to buy beans that day. He said he'd be back tomorrow. Then he rode off on his bicycle to his cousin's house. But instead of leaving the bike and catching a bus together, the cousin got on his bicycle, too. Together, they pedaled the 35 kilometers under the blistering March sun to Playa Celeste. In familiar places, Enrique was courageous, but Playa Celeste was out of his element, and Enrique was too timid to come alone. The cousin promised to keep the secret. Enrique promised to buy the beer.

They arrived while I was at work, rented a room in a pension across the street from the room I lived in, and came to find me at the real estate office where nothing ever happened.

At five o'clock, I left the office and the three of us went to a beach-front bar for a beer. We were nervous. Now that it didn't matter how Enrique and I acted together, we didn't know how to act. Luckily for us, the bar was setting up for a dance—the one thing we did know how to do together. So we danced. Playa Celeste was a small town in those days, and everyone fit into the same bar. Enrique and I danced there like we never could have anywhere else, unconcerned about who was watching. When the music ended sometime around midnight, we realized that Enrique's cousin was gone. Enrique put his arm brazenly around my waist and walked me home.

I led Enrique into my small suffocating room where he was first shy, then powerful. This was the night we'd been waiting for since January when he kissed me at dawn. My tiny bed was noisy in the quiet night, but there was no one to hear us. He tried to *get up and go back to the room across the street where his cousin was sleeping, but I asked him to stay. March is stifling hot even at night, so I opened the bedroom door to the misty ocean air and in moments, Enrique snored lightly by my side.*

In the morning, we all had breakfast together at a little restaurant and they pedaled home to Los Ríos to tell anyone who asked that the bean deal in the mountains fell through.

A LUCKY BREATH

I think about calling Rebeca.
It would be so wonderful to drink coffee with her, talk, tell her everything.
We could sit in the kitchen with Mami and Rebeca's daughter who is four.
We could watch stupid soap operas together and say which actor we think is the cutest.
Rebeca's little girl could get the brush and give me silly hairdos.
Rebeca could scold her for pulling my hair while I pretended it didn't hurt.
I want to call her but I am too ashamed.
She thinks I am in Atlanta with my sister.
My Costa Rican family and friends were so happy for me when I left for the USA.
They were so envious.
I can't tell them that I was unhappy there, and that I came back.
So many Costa Ricans dream of moving to America.
Coming back six weeks later to a miserable little apartment in San Francisco de Dos Ríos is thumbing my nose at their dreams.
I can't do it.
And then there's David.
I left my husband because I couldn't be the acquiescent wife he expected.
And what have I done but taken up with another man who is the same?
David doesn't cheat on me or shout at me, but if he listened to me at all he would comprehend that I don't love him.
He doesn't listen to me.
And if I tell Rebeca and her family that this new man I live

with, who is more like Enrique than not, is Nicaraguan, my humiliation will be complete.
This border-generated prejudice is not one that I share, but how can I tell the truth to Rebeca?
The real problem is not that I came back from the USA or that David is Nicaraguan, and I know it.
The problem is that this is all wrong.
I have gone from bad to worse.
I didn't mean it.
I don't know how it happened.
But everything is upside down.
I cannot face the people who love me.
So I hide.
I try to avoid places where I might see someone I recognize.
Or be seen.
I don't know that many people in San José, but I watch for them everywhere.

Guilt chokes me.
I realize that I am doing a terrible thing.
Without malice, in my confusion, I am cruel.
I allow David to believe that we are starting a life together when I know we aren't.
I feel sick.
I have to stop this.

I tell David I can't live with him anymore, can't be with him.
He cries.
I cry too, because I have so much to cry about.
He reminds me that this is what I said I wanted.
Did I?
Or did he hear that in my silence?
I don't know.

We are both crying.
I hate myself for this.
But we cannot live together, and I finally say so.
He says he will leave if I want him to.
I want him to.
I need him to.
He says he will leave tomorrow.

I don't think I believe him.
Where will he go?
He has no money and no job.
He says he's trying, and smokes more and more cigarettes while looking dejectedly at the newspaper.
I don't think he is trying.
I think he knows that when he gets a job, he will have to go.
I think he is pretending to try.

Days pass and David doesn't have a job.
He says he will leave, but he doesn't.
I say one of us must go.
He gives me his permission to leave if I want.
He says he will stay and take care of our apartment if I need some time away.
He is refusing to understand.
At night, he wants to make love.
I tell him no.
He torments me for hours.
I am tired and he won't let me sleep.
He doesn't force me, but he won't stop, and I am exhausted.
The easiest way to silence him is to give in.
Soon he is sleeping.
When he is snoring, I can think about what to do.
I open my mouth to say "get out" but no sound comes.

I was Mateo and Norma's roommate, not Enrique's wife, when I went with Mateo and Enrique to the mountain for curiol. Curiol is the word for the paints we used to color the pottery—rock pigment not for sale in any store, but hiding in veins at secret spots in certain mountains. Women don't go to collect curiol. Women stay home with the children. They stay home to prepare food for the men who go, and will return hungry. But I was a woman with no responsibilities, so when Mateo said to me, "Vamos," of course I went.

We collected curiol negro that day, at the most sacred of all the sacred places the ancestors went to gather colored stones. Mateo explained to me that when we climbed the mountain to the curiol site, we would not speak. It's bad luck. If you speak on the mountain with the black curiol, you frighten away the spirits that lead you to the curiol you need to earn your living, and the black veins hide in the flesh of the hills. Curiol negro is the hardest color to find, the one that lives only in the slimmest veins, only in the highest mountain which you can only get to on the hottest and driest days of the year. It was February 29, 1996.

Mateo and I got up at three in the morning and drank the hot coffee Norma made for us. We would want to be at the curiol site by daybreak in order to collect what we needed and leave the mountain before the sun became strong enough to harm us. In the morning cool, we didn't mind the long pants, shoes, and socks we needed to wear because of snakes we wouldn't be able to see in the dark. We wore long sleeves and hats to protect us from the eventual sun. In our backpacks we brought rice and bean lunches, and water. Enrique met us in front of the house.

Mateo, Enrique, and I rode our bicycles the three kilometers to the other side of Santa Cecilia under the stars and occasional *streetlight. Outside of town, we left the bikes lying hidden in the weeds by the barbed wire fence we climbed through, and set off on foot. It was dark. Mateo and Enrique wanted to run. Run, because even though it is blackest night, day is coming, and when day comes the sun will burn us through our clothes, we will drink our water, and the rocks we are touching will burn our fingers. I didn't know these things, but Mateo and Enrique knew them well. They ran, and I ran behind them through dark meadows with high grass. By starlight, we began to see the silhouette of the mountain ahead of us—the black space where no stars are. We ran stumbling, laughing in stifled hysterics about the dangers of snakes, angry bulls, and fresh cow pies. There was no road. Mateo and Enrique lead the way by landmarks: the trees, the rises, the gullies in the terrain. When we came to the fence on the other side of the pasture, we slipped carefully as felines between the strands of barbed wire and the climb began. Up and up as the sky paled above and around us.*

We climbed the steep tree-speckled slope of dry grass to a sudden cut where the earth has been clawed away and the raw mountain flesh stands pale in the sun. This was the secret place of the black curiol. Birds spoke around us, and the February winds picked up strength as the sun melted the night's coolness. We'd already drank half of our water, we were hungry, and the sun was cresting over the mountain top. We put down our packs in the shade of a tree and looked out over the dry valley below us. Above, a cloudless morning sky advised us not to waste time.

We brought tools with us. Both men wore machetes strapped to their waists, Enrique brought a small shovel, and each of us had a spoon.

I followed Mateo to a deep gash cut into the shoulder of the mountain. He reached into the shadowed space with his spoon and tapped the sandy white stone. It crumbled away to reveal more white flesh beneath. He demonstrated to me how to move the spoon carefully over the flaking rock, watching for black veins of gold to appear, speaking to me in undertones little more than a whisper. He showed me how to catch the black power in the spoon when it appeared in thin lines amidst the white. He poured the black powder from his spoon into a small plastic container that once contained Chinese food from a restaurant in Santa Cruz.

Enrique and I were not lovers then, but soon we would be. We stood side by side, working together in silence as the day got hotter, sweating, focusing our attention on the texture of tiny spoonfuls of mountain, gingerly tapping, deftly catching specks of black.

We used as few words as possible. This is where we would carve out the answer to our prayers for daily bread. Necessity assured our reverence. It was our task to find it, collect it, and carry it home to turn into rice, beans, electricity, a pair of sandals. There is no store that sells curiol, no other place this black dust can be obtained.

I felt the ancestors watching us as if they were my own. The sun blazed high, the water we drank evaporated from our skin, our bellies growled, and we decided to leave the mountain. Mateo and Enrique were satisfied with our container of black earth. My heart was both open and full.

A LUCKY BREATH

I decide to make the impossible phone call to Rebeca and Mami.
I will announce that I've come back to Costa Rica and am in San José.
They can think or say whatever they want.
I will tell them I need a place to stay.
I have to get away from David.
I will ask if I may rent Mami's extra bedroom until I find an apartment.
Mami needs the money and I need a place.
I don't have to tell her everything.
I will not tell her about Puntarenas or David or any of this mess.

Walking through the city center toward a public phone to make this call, I nearly collide with Mami.
Right there she stands in front of me, materialized from the multitude.
I am aghast.
My worst fear has just come true.
Both of us are shocked to speechlessness.
I stammer that I was going to a phone just now to call her.
I really was.
Her shock explodes into hurt that I've been in the city and didn't call immediately.
I try to appear calm, but I am talking too fast.
I explain that I need a place to stay, expecting her to insist that I come home.
Instead, Mami tells me that her sister has moved in, and the house has no empty rooms.

I listen to this devastating information, nod, smile, and promise to visit on my next day off.
In fact, I am destroyed.
Now I am homeless.
Or worse, I have a home that I cannot live in.
And I have nowhere to go but back there.
I put on my sunglasses so as I walk down the street no one can see I am crying.

When I get back to the apartment, David tells me he has wonderful news.
He says he got a job.
Right here at the building supply store where we live.
He is delighted.
He won't need bus money or packed lunches.
I feel sick.
If this is true, it means he won't leave the apartment.
I don't know if it is true.
I don't know if I hope it is, or hope it isn't.
The only thing I do know that I don't have to hide from my only friend Rebeca anymore.

I go to Rebeca's house, and over cups of coffee I tell her everything.
I don't mean to, but after I start the story I can't stop.
I tell her every humiliating detail.
I confess to her my trip to Nicaragua and my affair with David.
I tell her how lonely and cold I was in Atlanta.
She tells me I am crazy.
I tell her she's probably right.
But she pours me more coffee and offers me another piece of cake.
I tell her about the horrible house in Puntarenas.

A LUCKY BREATH

I tell her David followed me out of Puntarenas and lives with me now in San Francisco.
I tell her he won't leave.
He says he will, but he doesn't.
It is such a relief to have a friend—to tell the truth to someone, finally.
I haven't told the truth to anyone for a very long time.
I have so often been speechless.
I have told a thousand lies of omission.
The truth shocks even me when I tell it.
Rebeca convinces me that David is not going to move out.
Regardless of what I say or what he says.
Unless I force him to leave, he won't do it.
She lends me a thick green blanket because at night in San Francisco de Dos Ríos I am cold, and all my money is gone.

Rosita introduced me to Playa Celeste. She wanted to be my friend probably because I am a gringa and she thought I had money, not because we had a single thing in common. She could not have been more wrong about my finances. Maybe she hoped I would become her pimply son's novia. He spoke enough English to annoy me in two languages, which I didn't find attractive at all, but when Rosita invited me to the beach with them one day in early February, I went. The beach is the beach no matter what. She said we could go to Playa Celeste if I wanted and asked if I liked Playa Celeste. I said I didn't know. I'd never been there.

We rode to Playa Celeste in Rosita's dented orange Subaru Brat, parked in the shade, and set up a little charcoal grill. We swam in the blue bay, drank beer from the cooler she brought, and grilled thin slabs of meat over the fire. Rosita talked and talked. The more she talked, the less I wanted to be her friend, but I loved the beach. I decided I didn't care how much she talked or what she said as long as I could swim in the ocean and lay in the sand. It seemed like an acceptable exchange.

I wasn't looking for a job that day, but I got one. Rosita's friend who earned himself fat commissions tipping off real estate agents about properties for sale saw us eating in the shade. He talked almost as much as Rosita, which gave me a reprieve. Relieved of my labor of listening, I was deliciously dozing when I heard Rosita say my name. I opened my eyes and sat up. The office this man worked for, she said, was looking for a bilingual secretary. They needed someone who would answer the telephone, talk to potential clients that stopped by, and keep the contact list current. Rosita's friend asked if I could use a computer. My pulse sped up.

I didn't want to leave Los Ríos. I loved living with Mateo and Norma more than I'd ever loved living anywhere. I wanted to make clay beads on the shady porch with Mateo and Enrique every day for the rest of my life, stir gallo pinto over the wood fire with Norma, watch soccer practices in the late afternoons, and go to dances. I wanted to see Enrique every day.

But if I didn't earn money, it was going to collapse sooner or later. I would have to leave and go back to the USA. A job in Playa Celeste could be a solution of compromise. It would have been much worse to leave the country than to leave the town. I told Rosita's friend I was interested. Two days later I came back on the bus, interviewed, and took the job.

On Monday mornings, I took buses from Los Ríos to Playa Celeste. My new boss helped me find a room to rent above a deli by the beach. I handed over $200 a month for a room with a single bed and a window toward the ocean. Downstairs, in the deli, I could use the kitchen when the restaurant wasn't open. I stayed in Playa Celeste from Monday through Friday. My task was to stay within earshot of the phone that never rang in the real estate office. I waited for clients, wrote stories, and dreamed of weekends with Enrique. On Friday afternoons I rode anxiously home to Mateo and Norma's house praying to stay out of trouble, dreaming up ways to get into it.

Part VII: Tibás

I think about what to do, about how to stop living with David.
I break the problem into smaller pieces.
One of us has to go.
I think that although I can't make him leave, he also can't make me stay.
I am the one who must make something happen.
So I will do it.
I stop thinking about how to make David do what I want, and think about what I can do.
What my options are.
I do the only thing I can think of.
I buy a newspaper.
This time I'm not looking for apartments, which I could never afford, but for a room to rent.
A room with a door to close will be enough.
I need to get out of this apartment with David no matter what, no matter where I go.
I need to leave him on his own to resolve his problems.
I need to stop lying to myself and to everyone else.

If he will not go, I will.
I've done it before.
I can do it again.
Watch me.

I find an ad for a room that costs 40 dollars a month in a barrio called Tibás.
Tibás is across the city from San Francisco de Dos Ríos, much closer to work and not far from Rebeca.
David will never find me in Tibás.
No one will find me.
I make an appointment to see the room.
The woman on the phone tells me to wait outside the supermarket across from the bus stop at ten o'clock.
I take a bus to Tibás and wait exactly there.
The owner of the room, doña Viki, meets me and walks with me to her little house.
I like her.
She's a foreigner too, from Cuba, only a little older than I am.
Her home is a strange sad place where she lives alone, but the extra room is a price I can afford.
I don't care how strange or sad it is.
The next day I move in.
I don't know what I am doing.
I can't get inside my own head to think.
I bring only my clothes with me.
All my other things are in the apartment in San Francisco with David.
But I have to get out of there.
Things are just things, and I can worry about them later.
I have to do something and this is the only thing that occurs to me.
Maybe now I will be able to think.
I can decide what to do next, what's right and what's wrong.

I can lie on this tiny bed and wait until something makes sense.

My room in doña Viki's house is made of wood like the apartment in San Francisco.
It has a sad, sagging single bed, a lamp, and a nightstand.
That's all.
That's all there is space for in the tiny room.
I will have to live out of my suitcase.
I don't care.
Beside my room is Viki's room.
On the other side of Viki's room is the kitchen.
The kitchen has a 2-burner electric stove top, a sink, a few pots and pans, some dishes, a table, two chairs, and a refrigerator.
At least she has a refrigerator.
Life is so much easier when you have a refrigerator.
In San Francisco I don't even have a table or a chair, much less a refrigerator.
There is a bathroom.
The shower is cold, but Viki has a special Cuban invention for hot baths.
She shows me how to use it.
You fill a bucket with cold water from the shower.
Then you plug in this strange Cuban water heater.
It has a rubber handle and a metal coil that becomes red hot.
You put the metal coil in the bucket of water and be very careful not to touch the water with your fingers.
The water in the bucket becomes very hot, and you can scoop it over yourself with a cup that Viki keeps in the bathroom.
Hot bucket baths are another thing to be happy about.
San José's mountain water is frigid.
Outside is a back porch and a little yard.
On the porch is a sink for hand-washing clothes, and in the yard is a line for hanging them to dry.

A LUCKY BREATH

I have been back in Costa Rica for less than three weeks.
This is the third place I have lived.
I am not on the streets, but I am homeless.

I learned to make tortillas from Ana Luz, who lived in the house beside Mateo, Norma, and me. I loved to get up before dawn and walk through the damp darkness to her kitchen. The masa was always ready before I arrived, even in the morning dark, and the fire was hot under the comal. We worked in the screened kitchen behind the house, with the fire crackling beside us and the smoke wafting whichever way it wanted as dawn faded up over the sky and roosters crowed.

On several mornings each week, Ana Luz made piles of hot yellow tortillas. When she was done, she placed them in a clean bucket lined with a towel, covered them, set the bucket on her bicycle, and pushed it around the town selling the tortillas for coins. Ana Luz was married to Norma's father, a short fat man named Jesús, but she was in love with a tall dapper police officer from down the road. They both vehemently denied the rumors of their affair.

Ana Luz taught me to take the ball of masa and place it in the center of the round piece of plastic that would keep it from sticking to the wooden slab that was her work table. The slab had indentations worn in it from the hundreds of hand-turned pots Ana Luz made there, and the thousands of tortillas we pounded flat with our palms and pressed with our fingertips. She taught me to flatten the ball of masa first with the heel of my hand, turning it with quick flicks of my wrist like she did, then flattening my palm as the masa spread. She taught me to use two hands to keep the edges thick, and to pay attention to lumps and thin spots. Neither of us wanted me to ruin her reputation as the best tortilla-maker in Los Ríos.

Compared to Ana Luz, it took me forever to make a decent looking tortilla. She made three to my one, and cook them too, while I labored to make the edges right and the middle not too thin. But she loved the company of someone who didn't judge her, and I loved the company of someone I could tell the truth to about Enrique as the rumors about us began to eclipse all the others in Los Ríos. She paid me for my help with three hot tortillas to take home for breakfast when we finished, and with hours of friendship.

After I married Enrique and became part of the family, I made tortillas with María. When the corn in Martín's plots was ready, he picked it, shelled the ears, and soaked the kernels in water with ash. Angel ground it, then, in the hand-turned grinder, making an unbelievably delicious dough. As the sun sank low on windy summer afternoons, María tossed pale-barked sticks onto the cooking fire under the comal in the circular clay hornillo and cooked the tortillas we made. María marveled that I could make them well enough for them to puff with steam as they roasted. She poked affectionate fun at the other women and girls in the family whose tortillas remained flat on the comal.

I loved those evenings with María in the outdoor kitchen, hot yellow sunlight spilling in sideways over us. We gossiped affectionately about the neighbors and appreciatively complained about our husbands. I wasn't a foreigner during those hours. No one remembered my pale skin and oddly lilting accent; even I forgot them. We were just two women talking, cooking together over a fire, scolding children and dogs that ventured too close as the day melted into cool evening.

I wanted those afternoons to last forever. I wanted to never leave the circle of firelight, the crickets that sang, and María's rambling stories. I belonged. I promised myself anything was worth it. I would ignore Enrique's ill humors and bad behavior. In these places where he didn't belong, everything remained intact.

At night I realize why Viki's room is so cheap.
On the other side of my bedroom wall is a little restaurant that serves fried food until after midnight, and entertains its clients with a loud television.
I fall asleep to the clanging of pots, the wailing of women in the telenovelas, and the hearty laughter of people eating fried chicken and taquitos.
I dream that my room is full of mice that have gnawed their way up through the wooden floor.

Something is wrong with Viki.
She asks me a lot of questions in her strange breathy voice, then forgets the answers.
She stares at me, and follows me from room to room until I shut my door.
She uses my name in every sentence, either at the beginning or at the end.
Then she forgets it and asks me to tell her again what my name is.
I don't know what's wrong with her or how much of what she says is true.
She stares at me.
She makes me nervous.
Viki says she is married, but she lives alone.
She says her husband works for the electric company and has been assigned to a project in another part of the country.
She speaks with him on the telephone sometimes and talks about when she might go to visit him.
I think she is lying.
I think he is in jail.
Viki says she is a beautician.

A vanity with a mirror stands in the kitchen, but I never see clients come for Viki to cut their hair.
She invites me into her room to watch TV with her.
I say I am tired even though it is only 7 o'clock.
I go into my room and lie on the bed with the lights off, pretending to sleep, afraid she will knock.

When Viki isn't home, I cry.
And cry.
And cry.
I cry about Enrique.
I cry about the children.
I cry about María and Martín.
I cry because I don't know what to do.
I cry about leaving Michelle and everything I could have had in Atlanta.
I cry about David crying over me.
I cry because I am so disappointed with myself.
I cry because I am ashamed.
In the apartment I share with David, I cannot cry.
There is no place.
But I can do anything I want in my room behind the restaurant in Crazy Viki's house in Tibás.
I need to be alone, and here, at long last, I am.
So I cry.
For hours and days.
I am finally completely hidden.
I am nowhere.
I am no one.
No one notices me.
No one expects anything from me.
I have disappeared.
I am invisible.

Enrique first kissed me at dawn in the deserted bleachers of the bull-riding arena after a night of dancing at those yearly fiestas in Santa Cruz. He should have known, later, it's a place trouble can start.

During the week of revels, a noisy parade stumbles through the town every morning at sunrise, marking the end of one day and the beginning of the next. Especially because the parade is called "La Diana," I wanted to see it. I wanted to join in, just once—and I did. Enrique and I were among the handful of bleary-eyed folks from Los Ríos who stayed out all night with hundreds of other people drinking another beer, dancing to another song, eating roasted meat kabobs, drinking more, walking to another dance… I knew I would never be Enrique's girlfriend because he was a married man with children—but he was so much fun. So beautiful, impossible, and dangerous.

At 4:30 AM, the music throughout town suddenly went quiet. In the distance the wildly raucous marching band banged out a tenuous tune to an almost indistinguishable rhythm. It was La Diana. We'd made it to morning. Enrique grabbed my hand and pulled me, running with the stumbling crowd toward the last music in the last delicious drops of darkness. We threw ourselves into the drunken parade of revelers behind the drums, trumpets, and tubas, and danced through the streets at dawn with the disheveled throng. We were euphoric.

Then the night was over, everyone exhausted to the bone. Gray morning faded over the roofs of Santa Cruz as Enrique and I walked, hand in hand in front of everyone still awake, toward the bus stop. We were early. So Enrique led me up into the bleachers of the empty bull-riding arena and I followed. By the time he led me up those stairs by the hand, we had broken so many rules that one more didn't even matter. We were drunk, tired from dancing, and tired of resisting temptation. He sat. I sat beside him.

Enrique looked at me and sighed, "Ay mamita," in what can only have been resignation. We leaned together and neither of us tried to stop. We kissed while the sun slipped over the horizon. Enrique licked my lip. I fell in love.

Then the bus that would ferry us home to our breakfasts and our beds pulled up outside the arena. We hurried down the steps together trying to look separate.

After work, I go to visit David in the apartment in San Francisco de Dos Ríos.
He is home.
He says the job at the supply company fell through.
He says he will look for a different job.
He says he will move out of the apartment.
He asks me for money to buy food and cigarettes.
I give him money and I leave.
On the way back to my room in Tibás, I stop at a public phone in the city center and call Enrique.
I have to do it someday.
I decide today is the day.
Right now.
Each action I take on my own behalf makes me feel a little stronger.
Telling the truth to Rebeca.
Moving to Crazy Viki's house.
Now, I am calling Enrique.

There's only one telephone in Los Ríos, a public phone installed by the phone company in a private home.
The woman who lives in the home was born with a deformed leg, and her income is the coins neighbors pay her for the outgoing calls they make.
I dial her the number.
Her voice brightens with surprise and delight when she recognizes me on the line.
She will have new gossip to tell all who stop by for calls today.
I tell her I want to talk to Enrique.
I tell her I will call back in 30 minutes.
She will send one of her nephews spinning across town on his

bicycle to summon Enrique.
When I call back, Enrique is waiting by the phone.
I ask him how he is.
He asks me how I am.
I tell him I am in Costa Rica.
He is surprised.
I tell him congratulations on his new wife.
He says she is not his wife; I am his wife.
He thinks I have come back for him.
I tell him I have not.
I tell him I have come back for a divorce.
He says he wants to see me.
I know I must face him but I am afraid.
I am afraid of him.
I am afraid of me.
I am afraid he will find out about David.

If he finds out about David, he will be furious and call me a whore.
He will tell María and she will rub me out of her heart.
He will tell his children, and I will no longer be their father's wife.
I will be a dirty gringa.
Even though I was faithful while we were together and he was not.
The double standard for men and women is stark and non-negotiable.
Losing my husband is a terrible thing.
If I also lose his María, Martín, and the children, I won't be able to bear it.
I will gouge my eyes out.
I will claw through my own skin.
We agree to meet in Parque Central.
He must not find out where I live.

~~~

It was still the rainy season when, suddenly, the tap hissed air. All the taps in Los Ríos hissed air. Men hurried to the site of the well to see what happened and met the alarming electrical smell of melting wires. A check of the water level explained the problem—it was much too low.

We couldn't shower, brush our teeth, or wash our hands. We couldn't wash the dishes, but then we couldn't cook, either, other than frying platanos or eggs. There was no way to get a drink or give one to the thirsty chickens or dog. You could flush the toilet once. And it was no use you ask for water from the neighbors.

The town association called a mechanic to repair the pump, but the pump was failing and the well was failing. A well expert came. He peered into the hollow well, eyed the dying pump, and suggested that it only be used from 6 to 8 in the morning and from 6 to 8 at night. As the water level permitted.

I was a guest in Angelina's home, then—the first of my homes in Los Rios. She gave me the extra bed in her little boy's room, and scoops of rice and beans at mealtime. Angelina put a bucket in the pila in the kitchen. She cooked with the water she collected there. We washed our plates and forks and brushed our teeth. At 6 AM when the water came on, Angelina was already up turning yesterday's left-over rice and beans into today's gallo pinto for herself, her five sons, and me. She opened the taps to fill buckets and pans in the kitchen and in the bathroom. A bucket in the shower would provide a few scoops for washing for each of us. Another bucket by the toilet would be two flushes between morning and evening. Or whenever the water next flowed. Sometimes the long-awaited evening water never came. The most dreaded sound of all was the sound of nothing when you turned the tap at 6 PM. On those nights, all of us fell asleep thirsty, gritty, and got up in the night to pee outside the house in the shadows.

When the rainy season ended and the sky cleared, there was, as we had dreaded for months, no more water in the well. And for one week, in the heat of January, day after day, Los Ríos had no running water. The tiny town association called on every available government agency in a desperate search for funding, not only for a new pump, but for a new well.

I lived at Mateo and Norma's house, then, when the rains stopped and Los Ríos had no water. Things were a little easier there than they had been at Angelina's. There were half as many of us.

The old wells saved Los Ríos that week. Time cartwheeled backward one hundred years. Beside the wooden houses where grandmothers live, old hand-dug wells still held fresh clear water, potable and clean. Mateo's mother had a well beside her home on the other side of town. Norma and I walked there together several times a day swinging an empty bucket one way, then carrying it between us on the way back, switching sides when our fingers cramped and our shoulders burned.

Older women perched buckets of water on rolled towels on their heads. They ambled easily along, laughing and chatting as they walked. I envied that impossible-looking skill. At home, I practiced. I put a kettle on my head with a bag of rice inside for weight, but even that was a lost cause. Every three steps, I caught it as it fell. The fits of giggles that shook me didn't help. Norma laughed at me until she was wiping tears from her eyes. She could walk further with the kettle on her head than I, but not a lot. Mateo called us locas, and decided to show us how this woman's task is done. He held the kettle to his head with both hands and waltzed through the kitchen, hilariously swinging his hips and imaginary skirt.

There is faded photo of Norma and me walking down the road to Mateo's mother's house, each holding a handle of a burlap sack of dirty dishes. We tired of carrying water or waiting for Mateo to bring it to us, so we invented a new strategy: carry the dirty items to the water. The bag was heavy, but not as heavy as water. In the bags over our shoulders, are a change of clothes and our shampoo.

There is another photo of Norma and me at Mateo's mother's house washing our clothes in the pila beside the well, smiling widely. In the photo I am pulling a rope that holds a bucket of water I am drawing from the belly of the well.

That night, after dozens of buckets of water, we were not smiling as we prepared dinner, frying gallo pinto and sliced platanos over the fire behind the house. Our hands were blistered, our arms ached, and our knotted shoulders burned. Mateo's mother laughed at us that afternoon as our smiles faded to grimaces. She grew up this way and this is how she raised her children. She shook her head sympathetically at our helplessness, at our not knowing how to live without water magically flowing from taps.

Government funding appeared, and water flowed again from a new well through a strong new pump. All of us cheered, then sighed with relief. Norma and I cleaned the house, mopped the floor, and washed the clothes and pots and dishes in the sink on the back porch. Mateo bathed the dog. All on the same day, within a matter of hours. We felt so lucky, so privileged.

I stood under the decadent cool stream in the shower, letting the water pour through my hair, over my scalp, running in rivers over my body. Every breath was a prayer of gratitude.

A LUCKY BREATH

My teeth hurt.
They ache in my mouth in a way that I have never felt before.
I cannot afford to see a dentist, but I am afraid of what may be wrong with me, so I make an appointment anyway.
I don't know what a root canal is, but I've heard they are expensive and painful, and I hope I don't need one.
The dentist checks my teeth.
She says that nothing is wrong with any of them, says that I am grinding them in my sleep and asks me if I am experiencing stress.
I tell her yes.
She says I must stop grinding my teeth or I will ruin them.
I would like to ask her how.

I notice the dentist is right.
I wake in the night with my jaw clenched.
During the day, I realize that I am constantly biting down—while riding the bus, while at work, all the time.
I try to make myself relax my jaw, stop biting.
It lasts only seconds.
I put my tongue between my teeth.
Now I am biting my tongue which is painful, but I can't afford to destroy my teeth right now.
With the two rents I have paid, I can barely afford food.
In which case, maybe I don't need teeth so badly after all.

Enrique comes to the capital to see me.
We meet in Parque Central at noon, in the roaring center of the city.
He looks smaller than I remember him.

In my mind, he is fearsome and huge.
The man who meets me in the park seems small, old, and dry.
His skin is loose, and his eyes are dark.
We are kind to each other, heartbreakingly kind.
The last time I saw him he was riding away from our house in a red shirt, going to work.
Unsuspecting.
He says he wants me to come home.
He wants another chance.
I tell him there are no more chances.
We talk about how to divide our house and our things.
He waits for me to break.

When he comprehends that he cannot to change my mind, he stands up, takes my hand and pulls me through the streets.
He says we will find a lawyer now.
He says if you want a divorce, you will have a divorce.
I don't know where we are going.
I am nauseous, half-blinded by tears, and devastated by the comfort of feeling my hand in his.
He pulls me over the uneven sidewalks in his rough, familiar way.
I've learned to walk like this, like a dance, where my balance is so fully surrendered to him that if he lets me go, I will fall.
We blunder up one side-street and down another, over the cracked sidewalks of San José until we come to a door with an "Abogado" sign.
Enrique leads me in.
I am crying now.
The lawyer asks how he can help us.
Enrique looks at me.
Through my tears I say we have come to get a divorce.
The lawyer looks at Enrique.

Enrique says nothing.
The lawyer is confused.
He asks if I am sure.
I say yes I am sure.
I want a divorce.
I also want to cry.
Enrique waits for me to cave.
I insist through my tears.
I don't back down.
We answer the questions, sign the papers, the lawyer makes copies, and the process begins.

In Los Ríos, decent women don't drink. Yesenia drank, and Angelina told me Yesenia wasn't decent. Norma told me she wasn't decent. They cautioned me about drinking beer with Yesenia, but I never saw Yesenia do anything unbecoming. She would walk into a bar, order a beer and a small plate of food called a "boca," and talk to the other customers. It wasn't her fault they were always men. I never saw her do anything remotely indecent other than simply being there against the rules. I drank beer with Yesenia when she invited me, and I didn't care what anyone said.

Rumor had it that Yesenia's daughter Iris was Enrique's. This didn't bother me in the least—at first because I didn't know Enrique, and later because why should I be upset about a child conceived before I knew her parents? I couldn't see the logic. Yesenia said the rumor wasn't true, but her denial was unconvincing. It was all the same to me. I liked sitting in the bars with Yesenia once in a while, drinking beer until the room spun. Men bought us beer and told us we were beautiful. We smiled and drank, and when we were tired, we went home. Yesenia could drink an infinite amount of beer without ever getting the hiccups or starting to nod off at the table I like I would if I drank too much. Everyone frowned on my friendship with her, but I ignored them. If she in any way deserved her reputation, she never demonstrated it in front of me.

On New Year's Eve 1995, Yesenia and I went out on the town. She'd asked me a few days before if I wanted to go with her to the New Year's dance in Santa Cecilia. I was dying to go. My other choice was to stay home with Norma and either watch TV or go to church—the two things she did in her free time. Just before dark, I put on my bright-colored new dress, my new terribly-uncomfortable shoes, stuffed some money in my bra, and practically ran out the door. I felt beautiful.

A LUCKY BREATH

Yesenia and I sat on high wooden stools in the cantina across from the salon de baile in Santa Cecilia and drank the beers a fat guy named Orlando was buying for us. I wished we could buy our own beer because I wanted Orlando to go away, and as long as we were drinking the beer he was buying, he wouldn't. I hoped Enrique might come to Santa Cecilia, and if he did, I didn't want to be stuck owing another guy attention for having bought a bunch of beer. I wanted to drink with Enrique, and I wanted him to ask me to dance. I didn't care whether Yesenia's seven-year-old daughter was secretly their love child or not. I didn't care that he wasn't single. I didn't want to seduce him or cause anyone trouble—I just wanted to dance merengue and go home.

And then as if I'd summoned him, Enrique, flanked by a cousin of his who was always up for adventure, appeared in the doorway of the cantina where Yesenia and I nursed our beer buzzes. Enrique grinned with all his teeth. They were slightly slurring their syllables as they pulled up the last empty bar stools. Orlando quickly figured out he wasn't needed anymore, and he went to drink at a different bar. Enrique and his cousin sat down and bought another round of beer.

I don't remember what we talked about. I remember how I felt there, on the last day of the year I moved to Costa Rica, drunk in a scrappy bar in Santa Cecilia with Yesenia, Enrique, and sidekick. I was happy. I felt light as a butterfly. A live band pounded out merengues and cumbias in the salon across the street. Enrique and the cousin asked if we wanted to dance. Yesenia and I looked at each other. We pretended it didn't matter much to us if we went or not. But they said it was up to us to decide if we were going to dance or stay in the bar.

"Vamos?" I asked Yesenia. She got up from her barstool and we all walked out of the bar.

Later, when the 10-second countdown to midnight suddenly interrupted the music, I was dancing a dizzy merengue pressed *against Enrique's chest. I could barely breathe the way he pinned me to him, but he spun me so fast I would have fallen if he'd let me go. He didn't. A cheer went up at the end of the countdown, and everyone shouted, "¡Feliz Año!" and hugged and kissed whoever was near. Enrique hugged me and kissed me on the cheek. I kissed him back and said, "Feliz Año".*

Then the music started again. The dancing started, and the new year started.

Everything started, then.

I don't want to go to Crazy Viki's house because I don't want her to see my red eyes.
I don't want to tell her why I was crying.
So I go to visit David in San Francisco.
David is happy when I tell him about the divorce.
He is confused about why I would cry.
Isn't it what I wanted?
He tries to make me laugh.
He keeps saying "nosotros," talking about how much better things are going to be for us now.
I feel worse and I wish I wasn't here with him.
I wish I was nowhere.
I wish I was back in Los Ríos with Enrique, or in Atlanta with Michelle, or in Pennsylvania with my parents, or dead somewhere.
I wish I never existed in the first place.
I wish I was a dog with one bowl for food and one bowl for water.
I wish I was a cockroach hiding between the door frame and the wall.

I had a little white house with a yard and a clothes line, chickens, a dog, a washer, a refrigerator, a table, a television, and a husband.
María lived next door.
I had my closet and my clothes.
I had my kitchen and my plates.
I had fans and a couch.
I had a bookshelf.
I had a truck.

I had a cat.
Now I have nothing.
I don't know where I am.
I don't know what to do.
I have a dark miserable apartment I can't live in.
I have a room in the house of a crazy lady.
I have boxes of things.
I have a job where I sit at a desk in front of a computer.
The only time I know where I am is when I am on the bus going somewhere.
Then I know I am on the bus.
In a seat beside a total stranger.
The bus is better than the apartment or the room.
No one tries to talk to me on the bus, but I'm not alone, either.
There are warm and interesting strangers.
No one asks me anything.
All of us sit there and ride.
We are all ok.
On the bus, I know I won't go crazy.
I keep myself together because I am on the bus.

A LUCKY BREATH

The bottle of rum was half empty when Enrique walked through the door with it. If Norma had been at home, she wouldn't have let him in the house, but she had gone to a church committee meeting that afternoon. Mateo was burnishing pottery with a round stone, and I was waking up from a Sunday nap. We helped him finish the bottle.

Enrique wanted to go to a fiesta at a plaza on the outskirts of Santa Cruz. Mateo knew Norma was going to be mad about us drinking in the house, and he had an idea to solve both problems at once. He borrowed a little pick-up truck from a friend who owed him a favor, and when Norma came home, before she could draw a deep breath to start the sermon, he told her to get in. We went to Enrique's house to pick up Inez, and the five of us zoomed out of Los Ríos as the sun sank behind the mountains.

When we got to Santa Cruz, we parked by the plaza where we could eat stewed chicken and listen to a salsa band play. Inez and Norma dank orange fanta; Mateo, Enrique, and I drank beer. I pretended not to hear Norma and Inez grumbling about borrachos, rum, and beer. I pretended I was sober, which I wasn't.

Enrique wanted to go into the salon de baile to dance. I thought that was a fine idea even though I wasn't dressed for it. But Mateo shook his head, Inez rolled her eyes, and Norma snorted. We were not going into that dance with all those borrachos, she said, and besides, we didn't have any money. Which was true. So, we stood outside watching.

Enrique was a happy drunk when we left Los Ríos, but not when it was time to go home. He became obstinate. Mateo tried to convince him to get in the truck, but he refused. "Yo no me voy," he glowered, and stomped like an angry bull. Inez tried to order him into the truck, but he shouted at her to be quiet, and walked the other way. Norma called after him that we would leave without him. "Váyanse!" he shouted, then laughed. He was getting madder by the minute, wanting to stay in Santa Cruz with the lights and the music.

But we weren't leaving without him, so I took a turn trying to reason with him. I walked to him where he stood and said, "Venga Enrique. Ya nos vamos." And Enrique followed me to the cab of the truck like a puppy and climbed in. I got in beside him and shut the door: Mateo, Enrique, and me in the front, with the wives behind us in the bed of the truck. It should have been Inez beside him, not me. But I didn't think twice about it until later. Inez was mad at him anyway, and we three had been drinking together for hours. I knew when I got in the cab of the truck, sandwiching Enrique between Mateo and me, he would stay there.

We bumped along in the pickup truck, driving drunk slowly on curving dark roads. Enrique sighed and laid his head on my shoulder. Or did I do that? I don't remember. It was nothing.

It was something.

When he lifted his head and our eyes met, the look that passed between us broke every rule ever written, and even though we were both dizzy, we both remembered.

Things were different after that.

A LUCKY BREATH

David makes friends with a neighbor who also lives behind the building supply store.
This new friend installs pipes for the water company.
The friend says the water company is hiring.
David applies.
The water company hires him.
He must work for two weeks before he gets paid, and then he will have his own money.
David says he will move out of the apartment to live with the friend, that way I can come home.
This is good news and bad news.
It's good news because I don't want to live with Crazy Viki.
I want to live in my apartment.
It's bad news because David's friend is too close.
I can see his house from my doorway.
But I can't help where the friend lives, so I try not to worry about that.
A different house is better than the same house.

This is a terrible mess, but I am doing the best I can it.
Every day I start from where I am when I wake up.

The mess is entirely mine.
I made it myself.
This is what I tell myself:
Clean up the mess.
I am lost, but not completely.
I don't know where I am, but I know where I'm not.
I'm not in Puntarenas in the house with 15 relatives.
I'm not sleeping in a bed with David anymore.

I have a job.
I found Rebeca and told her the truth.
I called my husband, and met him face-to-face.
I signed the papers for a divorce.
I am beginning to do things right.
I only have $100 to my name, but I don't owe anybody anything.
I'm trying not to ruin my teeth.
I am stumbling and staggering, but I am moving forward.
I must believe that I am.

I make myself understand where I am and how I got here.
I review the story chapter by chapter, over and over.
I moved to Los Ríos after college.
I did this because I loved Costa Rica, and because there was a Boy.
The Boy did not choose me.
I fell in love with Enrique.
We married, and did the best we could.
I loved Enrique, but I left him because I also loved myself.
I went to Nicaragua with David.
I left David and went to Atlanta.
I could not live in Atlanta.
David met me when I returned to Costa Rica because I gave him the flight information.
I let him take me to Puntarenas.
I let him follow me to San José.
I have fed him and taken care of him.
I am responsible for all of this.
Now I must make things right.
One thing at a time.

Enrique calls me at work and says he wants to see me again.

A LUCKY BREATH

David calls me at work and says that he moved out.
I tell Crazy Viki that I am going back to my parents' house in America so she won't ask questions.
She wishes me well, very sorry for my failed marriage and broken heart.
I pack my suitcases and take them to Rebeca's house.
I don't believe David.
I wasn't born yesterday.
I think it might be a trap.
I ride the bus to San Francisco de Dos Ríos to see if David is telling the truth about moving out.
This time, he is.

What hurt my feelings the most is that Mateo and The Boy must have secretly planned it. One of them should have told me beforehand, but neither of them had the courage. It would have been nice not to have to swallow shock and surprise on top of a broken heart.

The Girl's mother was strict and mean, she lamented, and The Girl didn't want to live there anymore. Over and over, she asked The Boy to take her away—to take her to his house to live with him. Finally, he said, he ran out of excuses to keep stalling. He lived with his parents too, and they were kind. They would be happy to have a daughter-in-law in the home to cook for their oldest son, to wash his clothes, and to help with the cleaning and pottery making.

He said he had to do it. They were novios, he shrugged, which meant to everyone that when she was ready, marriage was his intent. The fact that her parents allowed her to have a novio who visited her on the front porch on Wednesday and Saturday evenings indicated that they approved of the eventual marriage. The Girl was only 14, and The Boy was not really a boy. He was 24 like me. I thought I was a little more enlightened than everyone else—until the day this news rippled through Los Ríos. In my mind, 14-year-old girls were children, but in Los Ríos anyone capable of conception is a woman.

Mateo helped him. Under the cover of night while The Girl's parents were at a church meeting, The Boy, The Girl, and Mateo walked across Los Ríos carrying her belongings from her house to his. There weren't that many things.

And then they were ajuntados—married without the documents. The priest who visited the little church in front of the plaza to perform mass once a week frowned on this non-sanctified version of marriage, but the arrangement was fully respected by the community.

    That was it. An endless story ended. I could stomach secretly seeing him if he had somehow gotten roped into humoring a silly girlfriend, but sleeping with someone else's husband is different. Even though I was there first. Even though I knew the Boy loved me—or for a time, he had. I understood that I'd been wrong about many things all along.
    I agreed to see him again because I wanted to talk. He told her he was going night-fishing and came, one last time, to me in my room at Mateo and Norma's house.
    I asked him how it was going.
    He said it was going alright.
    I asked if he was happy.
    He said yes.
    I told him this would be our last secret meeting.
    He said, why?
    I said because you can't have both of us.
    He said, but until now I did.
    I said, yes you did, but now you won't.
    That was our last night together, ever. We'd loved each other for years, and the love wasn't gone but neither could it continue.
    The sadness that pressed down on us as we separated on the following gray dawn was as heavy as the water at the bottom of the ocean.

Part VIII: A Solid Door

I put the key in the door of my sorry apartment and push it open.
David's things are gone and there is a sad terrible letter in his nearly-illegible scrawl.
A love letter.
I am a heartless bitch, I think.
Two humans are torn apart because of me.
I am in shreds, myself.
I gather my things from Rebeca's house and bring them back to my apartment.
I have moved so many times in the last month that when I wake up in the morning I don't know where I am.

For a few delightful hours, I am happy.
I hang my clothes back in my closet and open the green blanket over my bed.
I am putting my suitcases away and humming, when David comes up the stairs.
He can see my doorway from where he lives.

A LUCKY BREATH

He has been watching me the whole time.
He says he needs money.
He is working, but it will be another week until he receives pay.
I give him some money so he can eat and smoke.
If I don't do it, he won't go away.
He tells me that with his first paycheck, he will take me out dancing.
He says we will drink and have fun like we used to do.
We used to have so much fun.
Everything used to be different.
I say, "Está bien," because I want him to go away.
I want him out of the house.
He assures me that everything will be okay, and that we will be together forever.
He tries to kiss me.
I say goodnight and make him leave.

At 5 in the morning, a knock on the door awakens me.
I ignore it.
I know who it is.
He knocks again.
I know what he wants.

But I have no more money for him, no more love, and precious little friendship.
I lie still as death and try not to breathe.
I don't move a muscle until long after the knocking stops and I hear his boots walk down the stairs.

I come home from work and leave the door to the stuffy apartment open to the evening air.
Within minutes, a pair of boots comes thumping up the stairs.
David stands in the doorway.

He is drunk.
I come out because I don't want him to come in.
He tries to kiss me.
I hold him back.
He whines and begs.
Even though it is early evening, I tell him I am tired and I am going to bed.
He tries to come in, but I pull the door shut behind me.
I turn off the lights and sit on my bed in the dark.
After the boots have gone back down the stairs, I turn on the light in the bathroom and prepare myself something to eat in the shadowy kitchen.

The next morning, David is knocking on the door again and this time he doesn't stop.
Through the door, I ask him what he wants.
He says he needs money for the bus.
Three more days until he gets paid.
I open the door, give him the money, and close it again.
This is not working for me.
When I asked him to move out, this is not what I had in mind.

 For six months, I lived in Angelina's house, then Mateo and Norma invited me to move to their home. I was delighted. They had no children, so at their house I had my own room.

 Mateo and I became friends almost before we could speak to each other, back when I first found myself in Los Ríos. I arrived for a three-month Study Abroad term with a hearty curiosity but very stumbling Spanish. Mateo was a neighbor, and my age. He rode down the dusty street in front of my host family's home on the strangest bicycle I'd ever seen— something he'd invented out of pieces of other bicycles, and, miraculously, it worked. The seat stuck up further than the handlebars, and the wheels weren't the same size. But he'd learned to stay on it. With his wide smile and the sharp mullet haircut that was several years out of style in the rest of the world, Mateo on that bicycle made me burst into laughter.

 He stopped the bike and said hello. He asked if I liked the bicycle. I said yes very much. He asked if I know how to ride a bike. I tried to tell him yes but only a normal bike. He laughed with his head thrown back and all of his teeth in the air. Matteo and I clicked instantly. Through the beginning Spanish I stammered back then, Mateo caught my sarcastic sense of humor and my limitless love of adventure. A lifelong friendship sparked. I came back four years later hoping to stay, and found him married to a vivacious young woman I immediately liked.

 Norma was a fierce housekeeper. At nineteen, she had already been married to Mateo for several years. She went to the University on Saturdays to study education, and helped Mateo with his pottery as time allowed. With Norma, there was never a dull moment, nor an idle one. She had an opinion about everything and everybody, which she shared without a second thought. It was a joy to bask in the warm sunshine of Norma's approval. I loved to detonate her explosive laugh.

Mateo and Norma always had enough to eat, and always something extra to go along with our rice and beans. Sometimes it was as simple as an egg, a slice of tomato, or a piece of bread, but after six months at Angelina's house with her five sons, even those things were luxuries I'd dreamed of at night.

Norma taught me to cook. She taught me everything I needed to know about how to be a woman in Los Ríos. She showed me how to use the electric rice maker to make rice seasoned with onion, cilantro, and sweet peppers. From her, I learned the trick of rinsing the starchy rice until the water runs clear before cooking it. The grains need to be loose, not sticky, in order for gallo pinto to come out right. Nearly everything else, we cooked outside on the wood burning *hornilla* under a low tin roof behind the house. This is where we boiled beans, made gallo pinto, and fried prestiños on rainy afternoons. I learned to use the hatchet and the machete to split kindling for our cooking fire. Norma taught me how to regulate the temperature by rearranging the pieces of wood. I learned that if you re-boil the pot of beans after every time you put a spoon in it to scoop some out for a meal, you don't need to keep the pot in the refrigerator. This came in handy when I lived in Santa Cruz with Enrique before we were married and had nothing but a two-burner stove top and a bed.

Having my own room meant a lot more than just having personal space—it meant no more sneaking to the abandoned house with The Boy. He and Mateo were practically brothers, and he was always welcome under their roof. He could send a message with Mateo if it was a good night to slip away unnoticed, and I could be certain to be found at home. Norma and I toyed with ways to facilitate The Girl finding out about these nights. She would have to break up with him then, and the silliness would be over. Everything might have gone differently if it had happened. Or maybe he would have said he was sorry and she would have forgiven him and nothing would have changed. We didn't get a chance to find out.

A LUCKY BREATH

Enrique worked with Mateo. He came to the house in the morning to burnish pots with a stone or a piece of a plastic bottle when Mateo had big orders to fill, then they split the profit. I made pottery too—beads for necklaces that nobody believed tourists would pay the equivalent of $10 for, but they did.

At first, Enrique was so shy in my presence that he wouldn't look at me. He wouldn't eat in front of me. At lunch time, instead of sitting at the table with the rest of us, he took his plate to the front porch and ate his meal there. I teased him because he was funny and cute. He laughed sheepishly without looking up. He looked at me other times, though. I watched him out of the corner of my eye.

Enrique complained to us that Inez didn't like him, that she constantly criticized him and argued about everything. He spent as much time as he could at our house because he didn't like being home, he said, and went back at night to sleep in the bed with the children. That's what he told us.

I spent cool mornings and windy late-afternoons cooking with Norma, and the hours in between etching and burnishing beads with Mateo and Enrique all through that first dry season, before Enrique and I fell in love and Norma couldn't be my friend anymore.

David receives his first paycheck.
While I am at work that day, I am nervous because I know he will come for me in the evening.
He promised to take me on a date and I do not doubt that this promise he will keep.
He says he wants to repay me for all the favors I have done him.
I know he hopes that if we drink, I will let him come home with me.
I know I won't.
There are not enough drinks in the universe to make me let him into my home or my bed.
But for me to refuse this invitation would be an insult to him.
I don't have the heart to do it.
Enough causing people pain.
It is impossible to politely refuse.
Common sense loudly tells me not to go, yet I must.
I don't know what to do.
Lie and say I am sick?
Then he will try to come in, and I don't want that.
Spend the night at Rebeca's?
No matter where I hide, he will be here when I get back.
He will be watching my door, waiting for me to come home.
I don't know where we will go or how I will stay in control of the situation.

I stall.
After work, I go shopping.
I can't hide forever, but I can buy a little time.
I buy some more things for my apartment: a pillow for my bed, two plastic chairs, and a mirror.

Until today, I have used a folded sweater as a pillow.
I have eaten standing or sitting on the floor.
Now I will have a pillow for my head, a place to sit to eat or read, and be able to look myself in the face.

It's six o'clock when I arrive home with my pillow, chairs, and mirror.
I am feeling strong.
I drop off my purchases and go to the little grocery store to buy eggs for dinner.
As I reach my stairway, I am suddenly face to face with David.
He is elated.
He has come to get me for our evening out.
He is ready, he says.
He is staggering drunk.
He invites me to join him at the neighborhood bar.
I stall again.
He is so drunk, the words are slurred.
I tell him I want to shower and eat, then I will meet him there.
He accepts this and returns to the bar.

I climb the stairs to my door in a cold sweat.
I feel as if bugs are crawling all over me.
I see Enrique when he was drunk, and how he and David are so much the same.
Through a mixture of fear and revulsion, I tack into the storm.
I can't run away from this.
I can't hide.
I am strong enough.
I am well enough.
Everything will be ok.
The worst is over, I tell myself, because I am no longer in love—not with David or with anyone else.

Therefore no one can hurt me.
I won't allow it.

I do exactly what I said I would do.
I eat.
I shower.
I promise myself that I will be friendly and polite.
David deserves the dignity of being allowed to buy me a beer if he wants to, after everything he had to ask me for.
Maybe it will be fun.
I don't see how, but maybe.

The bar is full of rough men with rough lives celebrating payday in their rough way.
I walk in easily because I've been in bars like this many times.
David leaps off the barstool when he sees me, stumbles, hugs me, kisses me, and loudly orders me beer.
I take the bar stool beside him.
The other drinkers leer at me.
I smile sweetly.
I know how to do this.
The stereo is wailing ranchera songs about betrayals and heartbreaks.
Some of the drinkers are trying to sing along.
I think David and I are going to have a conversation, but we don't.
We can't.
He is barely coherent.
He slurs to me that he loves me, tells me he wants me to be the mother of his children, promises he will wait for me forever.
His beer is gone before mine and he orders us each another.
I try to make small talk.
I tell him about my day at work.

A LUCKY BREATH

I tell him about anything I can think of.
So he won't talk about the future.
He isn't listening.
He tells me again that he loves me.

My shoes melted on the two kilometer walk home from Santa Cecilia. Growing up in Pennsylvania, I knew about sunburn, but I didn't know about melting soles and blistered feet. The pavement in Guanacaste at mid-day under the dry-season sun becomes almost a liquid.

They were cheap sandals. I bought them in the market in San José because I had very little money to spend, and the ones I brought with me from the USA were old and haggard. Their light weight felt comfortable, and I thought they would be the right thing for a hot walk home to Los Ríos from Santa Cecilia at midday. I didn't have to throw the shoes away, but the soles were uneven after that, and I never wore them out of Los Ríos. Just in case I had to walk back.

In those days, almost no one had a car. Any time we needed to buy something other than rice, beans, or coffee, we took the 7:30 AM bus to Santa Cruz by way of Santa Cecilia. The two options for getting home to Los Ríos were either to take the noon bus to Santa Cecilia and make the last two kilometers of the journey on foot, or to take the late afternoon bus that rolled through Los Ríos just before 4:00 PM. We usually chose the walk. There's nothing to do all day in Santa Cruz, especially if you haven't got money to spend. None of us had money to spend.

Most likely, I'd taken the bus to Santa Cruz to mail letters. I probably bought shampoo and maybe a few questionable tomatoes. I craved tomatoes so much in those first monhs. I felt independent. I knew my way around Santa Cruz, knew the language well enough to ask for what I wanted, knew which grocery store had the best prices, and knew to get in line early for a seat on the bus. I knew to wear a hat to protect my white nose and cheeks from the sun. I didn't know the fate of thin-soled sandals from the Mercado

Central on the noon walk from Santa Cecilia to Los Ríos, but I found out.

It was a long time ago, back in the beginning when I lived with Angelina and shared a room with her nine-year-old. I still had extra toothpaste and feminine hygiene products that I'd brought from the USA in the suitcase under my bed. I hadn't fallen for Enrique yet—I was still sneaking off at night to the tumble-down house no one lived in to meet The Boy I believed would choose me. I had $500 in travelers checks and a ticket home I would never use. Every day I learned a new word in Spanish, understood another figure of speech, deciphered a little more of the flow of sounds coming from radios and televisions.

There are moments of discomfort that bring about epiphanies. The day my shoes melted was one of them. There are lessons about humility. It was that, too. There are experiences that belong only to the rich, and those that belong only to the poor. This was neither. Blistering your feet through the thin sandals you chose as your walking shoes is one experience that belongs to someone who is falling through the cracks between categories.

Halfway through my second beer I get up and go into the bathroom.
I need to think.
This is worse than I imagined.
It's only 8 o'clock, and David is drunk out of his mind.
We aren't going to have fun tonight.
We aren't going to go dancing like we used to.
We aren't going anywhere.
This is a nightmare.
I need to get out of here, but how?
I cannot drink more than the rest of that second beer, but David will order me another any minute.
This is a mess—maybe a dangerous mess—and I need to be clear-minded.
David thinks he is going to spend the night with me, but he isn't.
No matter what I drink, he isn't.
But for the first time since I met David, I am afraid of him.
How am I going to get away from him?
What if he tries to rape me?
Normally, he wouldn't, but at this moment I don't know who he is.
I don't know what he would or wouldn't do.

This situation is out of control.
This night is out of control.
My life is out of control.
But I am still sober and I can decide to behave sanely.
In the midst of this insanity, I can still choose.
I breathe.

I look at myself in the dirty bathroom mirror—stare at myself in the eyes.
I say to myself that I am not having fun.
That I am not going to get drunk tonight.
That when I have finished the beer that is sitting on the bar, I am going to get up and go home.
Walk out.
No matter what.
I promise me this.
David will be shocked and offended.
But I am going home.
It's rude of me to leave, but it's rude of him to be drunk.
What can he do?
He can't physically stop me from leaving.
We're in a public place.

I take a deep breath, pray to God for strength, and walk out of the bathroom back to my barstool.

Three months after I arrived in Los Ríos, I took a trip to Nicaragua. A Costa Rican tourist visa is only valid for three months, after which you must leave the country or pay a fine when you do. You could be deported if you are caught with an expired visa. I didn't want to risk either of those things, so I obeyed the law: I left the country for 72 hours. The law doesn't say you have to go home; it says you have to leave. So I put $50 in my pocket and took a bus to Santa Cruz, then to Liberia, then north.

On the bus I clutched my backpack nervously, hoping to end up by nightfall in a town called Rivas. Norma told me it's not too far across the border and that it would be easy to find. Not that she'd ever been there. I had no idea what to expect at the border crossing. I had no idea what to expect, period. Nicaragua, to me, was a name from the evening news, with gunshots echoing in the background and dangerous rebels. The war was over, but it wasn't the war that made my hands clammy. I was afraid of fierce border guards, unhelpful officials, long lines, questions I didn't have the answers to, thieves, ill-intentioned taxi drivers, and the unknown in general.

I didn't know Enrique, then. He was just another man in Los Ríos whose name I'd learned. A handsome man, with long curls and beautiful eyes, who liked to sit under the tamarindo tree in the evenings with the other men, and who got hilariously drunk at the July 25th festival.

As I traveled, my mind busily puzzled out what to do about The Boy. I'd thought he meant it was over when he told me he had a novia, but it wasn't like that at all. The girlfriend he walked around the plaza holding hands with was hardly more than a child. She'd told her brothers that she liked him, he explained, and the only honorable thing to do was to become her novio. She was a bashful, pretty girl. And if a woman offers, a man accepts. It's a rule. Now he didn't want to hurt her feelings or infuriate the brothers. He said he loved me, and he didn't know what to do.

We became lovers almost immediately. It was inevitable. And complicated. Both of us had questions; neither one of us had answers. But we had loved each other already through so much space and time that, finally being together, there was no other way. I was sure he would tire of the little girlfriend silliness. We frequented a secret meeting place for nights that child could not imagine. Looking at her, I could barely summon jealousy. I wondered what would happen, how long he would keep up the charade.

The endless coast of Lake Nicaragua came into view from where I sat on the bus. I stared through the window as we bumped along, trying to remember anything I might have learned about it in school. And then something enormous and ghostly was suddenly materializing through the mist above the lake. I sucked in my breath. A towering triangle. A mountain. I understood I was eye to eye with a volcano. Up ahead, rising silently out of this fresh-water sea, stood a single tremendous mountain that swept upward in a perfect cone. At the top of this peak, sat a swirling cloud formed by the steam it exhales. As the bus bounced along the lake road, the mountain grew larger. I couldn't look away.

I wanted to go to the mountain, to touch the earth of its terrifying cone. I sensed life and death, destruction and creation, embodied by this one form that grew more solid before me as we neared it. I didn't know its name, but I would find it. I didn't know that the volcanic island contained roads and small cities, but I would learn. I didn't know one day I would sleep in the skirts of this cone as it stood among the stars, but I felt it call me in a language I understood without being able to speak it.

I finish my beer.
I set the bottle down.
I pull my keys from my pocket because I want them in my hand.
I say to David, "Gracias.
Tengo que trabajar mañana.
Voy para la casa.
Buenas noches."
I lean over and give him the customary kiss on the cheek, get up, and walk toward the door.
It takes a moment for him to understand.
He begins:
"Diana.
Espere.
Un momentito.
¡Espérese!
¡Una más y después nos vamos!
Diana!"

I am in the doorway and I don't turn around.
On the street, I start to walk faster.
I want to run but something tells me, "Do not run."
I walk as fast as I can.
It comes again: "Diana!"
He is in the doorway of the bar.
"Diana!"
I don't turn around.
"Diana!!"
He is out of the bar and coming behind me.

Walk, don't run.
Walk, don't run.
Only a few more steps to the gate of the building supply store and then I will be around the corner.
Not safe, but out of view.
Then, I can run.
"Wait!!"
He is drunk and closing in on me.

The gate is unlocked.
I close it after me and break into a run.
It's not very far to the stairs which lead to my door behind which is safety.
I sprint for my stairway, weak with terror.
The gate opens and slams behind me.
David is inside, running too.
His boots are running and he is screaming at me even though there are neighbors.
I run past the other apartments, around the corner and up my stairs.
Never, never in my life have I run from a drunken man and I know right now that I never will again.
My key goes into the lock, and I hear him turn the corner.
He spots me opening my door and screams my name again.
His boots are pounding up my stairs as I slam the door behind me and bolt it.

I can't breathe.
My heart is pounding so fast I think I am going to faint.
He is on the landing outside the door.
I slide my shoes off, go into my bedroom and lock that door too.
I am hiding in the dark in my apartment and David is outside beating on the door.

"Diana!!" he roars.
"Abra la puerta!
Abra la puerta!"
I don't move.
He throws himself against the door.
"Diana!"
What will he do to me if the door doesn't hold?
It will hold.
It has to hold.
He is drunk and I am hiding in the corner of my dark apartment at the back of a building supplier, so scared I can hardly breathe.
What have I done?
What in God's name am I doing?
This is not my life.
This is a scene from a movie, from somebody else's life.
He kicks the door with his boots, the beautiful boots I bought him in the market in Nicaragua.
I remember the sound of my bathroom door in Los Ríos when it gave in to Enrique's boots that day.
Is this one stronger?
He screams.
His boots crash against the door.
I listen to the door hold.
He shouts my name again and again.
I am scared to move.
Scared to breathe.
A neighbor man comes out from somewhere and tells David I'm not there.
David shouts at the man that I am there and tries to start a fight with him.
The man goes away.
The beating and kicking continue.

I think about what I will do if the door begins to give.
The bedroom has a window.
Below the window are the rooftops of adjoining apartments.
I can squeeze out the window while he breaks the bedroom door and run across the other roof.
I can jump to the ground and run down the street.
I don't know where I will run to, but I am sober and David is drunk.
I'll think of something.
He can break things, but he can't outsmart me.
I kick myself for leaving my shoes in the living room.
If I have to run away, I will be barefooted.

The fury begins to subside, and I know I am safe.
For now, I am safe.
There are pauses now between the shouts and blows to the door.
David knows that I am not coming out.
I sit on my new chair and look around my room in the dim streetlight that filters through the only window.
Thank God it is the only window.
Thank God, thank God, thank God.
I wait for a long time without moving a muscle until I hear the boots go back down the stairs.

I learned that the rainy season in Los Ríos is the lean season. The school paid my host family to feed me when I was a student, so while I experienced simplicity, I did not experience actual need. Simplicity and shortage can appear similar, even indistinguishable, on the outside. But they feel different in the belly.

When I arrived at Angelina's house at the beginning of May, the rainy season of what turned out to be a very wet year had already started. We all made pottery every day that we could, but often the intense humidity made it impossible to work on the damp clay. And as the season progressed, fewer and fewer tourists came to buy our pottery. It was our only income.

At Angelina's house none of us went hungry, but fed almost exclusively on rice and boiled beans, I craved vegetables. At night I dreamed of tomatoes. I craved chicken. I craved bread. I craved milk. I craved everything. I could have cried for joy at the taste of a fried egg.

Angelina's sons made gentle fun of me for not knowing how to cook rice, beans, or meat over an open flame, but no one offered to teach me. I didn't ask to learn. We couldn't afford for me to make a mistake that could cost us something to eat.

I could have bought myself the foods that I craved, but it would be rude not to buy enough for everyone. None of us earned enough money for that. I used the money I earned selling my pottery to buy bags of rice, beans, bottles of oil, coffee, salt, and sugar. When I brought home a pineapple, hungry for a juicy slice, Angelina chopped and blended it into a sugary beverage. So I stopped buying fruit. I bought canned tuna. Eggs. A chunk of fresh cheese, sometimes. I nibbled slices of avocado sprinkled with salt as if they were a rich dessert, making the flavor last.

I didn't mind about the bruised spots on bananas anymore, or if they were overripe or even a bit black. I ate the strings I'd always removed in disgust and sampled the bitter peel when no one was looking. I hated myself for the stupid ungrateful days of my life when I ignorantly threw away browning bananas, the skin of chicken, the crust end of loaves of bread, the perfectly chewable gristle of meat. When one of the five sons brought an armadillo home from a successful hunt, I chewed and gulped that rodent's flesh in delighted gratitude.

Local conventional wisdom holds that sleeping on your stomach dulls hunger. I tried it, and it seemed to work. The rainy season that first year was long, and none of us sold enough pottery. We ate as little as we could.

I learned the hard way to get up early for breakfast because, whereas I would never ever have scraped the gallo pinto pot clean leaving nothing for anyone else, the five hungry brothers would. I rose almost in the dark on days when the rain clouds hung low and heavy, for a cup of sugary black coffee and a greasy scoop of rice and beans. We ate as reverently as a religious rite while the solid sound of falling rain pressed down on us from the tin roof. I stopped craving anything but one more spoonful.

I breathe a small sigh of relief.
Small, because David could come back.
If he does, he will be more drunk than he is now.
I prepare for the worst.
I fetch my shoes from the living room and re-bolt my bedroom door.

I empty my wallet into one of my back pockets and put my keys in the other.
I crawl into my bed wearing everything but my shoes and lie with my head on my new pillow.
If he comes back, I will be ready.
I lie awake for a long time, listening.
I'm not sleepy.
The fog in my brain lifts a little and things click into focus.
I understand.
I've almost forgotten what it feels like to understand anything.
And I still don't understand everything, but I do understand this:
THIS IS NOT MY LIFE.

I didn't leave Enrique for this.
I didn't leave Atlanta for this.
I left the beautiful family farm of my childhood for college, then I left my college degree and budding career for the magical country of Costa Rica.
But not for this.
Not to hide from a drunken man who is kicking my door because he thinks he loves me.
No.

No, no, no.
This is not my life.
I lie in my bed dressed to flee and I know this is not my life.
I have no one to blame for this but myself.
Look what I have done.
Look where I am.
I have erred, and gravely.
Now I am going to stop.
I am going to stop living this life.
I have asked David to leave me, and he won't.
I was wrong to allow him here in the first place, but even considering my mistakes, I don't deserve this.
This is too much.
I will not hide in fear, saved by a solid door.
Not.
Ever.
Again.

It is my father who comes to me now in my mind, my daddy who raised me to expect so much more than this.
A loving man.
A kind and humble God-fearing man who never shouted at his children or at his wife.
He disciplined me, but never in rage.
He guided me in gentleness and taught me I can do anything.
Including leave home alone.
Including take care of myself.
Including not accept this.
My father comes to me on this fearful night to give me courage.
He is with me.

I cannot sleep.
I am too angry.

I am too happy.
I am full of too much determination.
The smothering guilt I have carried melts away in the dark.
I hit the bottom and push off toward the surface, toward the light.
I know I have hurt David.
I have hurt Enrique.
I have hurt myself.
I have hurt everyone.
Tonight I have paid the bill.
And I forgive me.
I know what to do.
Yes, I do.
In the morning, you will see.

A LUCKY BREATH

❧

 Washing clothes is women's work. This is not because it is considered easy or of low value. Scrubbing the clothes of potters by hand in a cement sink is difficult and important, especially when money is scarce and clothing isn't easily obtained or replaced. Men cut and carry the wood for cooking fires and use machetes to trim tall grass where snakes might like to live. No one's job is easy.

 On my first visit to Los Ríos, my host mother washed my clothes for me, but when I came back on my own, I needed to learn to take care of myself. Some families had small semi-automatic washers, but Angelina didn't. Angelina had Juanita, the washerwoman, who came to the house to scrub the clothes of the five sons by hand in the cement wash sink in the kitchen.

 Juanita came to the house twice a week, and I studied her work. I watched how she wet the clothes by pouring water over them with a jícaro shell, sprinkled them with powdered soap and scrubbed—deftly rolling and unrolling each piece against the rough surface. I watched her rinse the garments with scoops of fresh water from the jícaro, beat them up and down, then wring them hard with her muscled arms. Juanita spoke with the voice of an animal, in grunts and torrents of half-pronounced words that, at first, I did not understand. She moved as if she were about to run away. Juanita's undomesticated five-year-old daughter shadowed her, scratched and stole, grunted, screamed, and copied her mother's nearly-unintelligible speech. All of us were poor, then, but Juanita and her little girl were the poorest.

 The child tormented the chickens, Juanita washed, and I gradually learned to understand their garbled Spanish. The payment for Juanita's work was the plates piled with rice and beans that she and her daughter devoured at midday. I watched them. They watched me. Juanita offered to wash my clothes for a small fee. I *said no. She shook her head in disgust at my stinginess, unable to comprehend my compunction to learn.*

She watched me struggle with the jícaro and the shirts, frowning at my sloppiness. Angelina's sons came to lean on the doorframe and watch me slap my shorts against the sink, imitating Juanita. They laughed at my clumsy movements and teased me about my raw knuckles. Neighbors who wandered by stopped and came inside to witness the spectacle of me washing.

A gringa washing by hand? Who knew it was possible?

I persisted. I ignored their merry mockery. I got faster and more efficient. As the weeks passed, the show became less entertaining.

A LUCKY BREATH

In the morning after that horrible night, I get up very early and leave my apartment.
David will still be sleeping.
I buy a newspaper and take the bus downtown.
I sit in the park looking for apartments in the newspaper.
I find one I think I can afford.
I call the number from a public phone.
The owner of the apartment says I can come see it now.
I get on a bus right away.
The apartment is in a neighborhood near Rebeca's house.
It is empty of appliances and furniture the way all rental apartments are in the city.
But it's being newly painted, it has a pretty tile floor, and four giant windows.
A fence of tall iron bars surrounds the property.
I pay the deposit for it.
The owner says I have to wait five days before I may move in.
I'd rather move today, but I can wait.
I can do anything.
I feel dangerously strong.
This is my life.
I tried to start over, and I got it all wrong.
But I can try again.
I can start over as many times as I need to.
This time, I will do it right.
I get on the bus and go to work.

The next morning at dawn, a knock on the door wakes me.
I open it.
There stands David, looking sheepish.
I don't smile.

He laughs nervously.
I ask him what's funny.
He says he was remembering the other night.
I say it wasn't funny.
He asks me why I didn't open the door.
I say I didn't open it because I don't want to talk to him when he is that drunk.
He tries again to laugh.
I ask him if he needs something.
He says he was mugged and that all his money was stolen.
I don't believe him for one second.
He drank the money.
I feel like smiling because I have a new apartment with windows, but I don't tell him.
I will start over one more time, and this time I will take no one with me.
No one.
I give him bread and coffee so he will leave me alone.

On my last morning in the apartment behind the building supply store, a knock on the door wakes me at 5:00 AM.
I open it.
David is on my porch.
Smiling.
He says that his key is lost and he needs to borrow my key to unlock the front gate.
This is a lie and I know it, an excuse to see me.
Does he think this will go on forever?
This is the day it will stop.
I don't tell him.
I lend him the key for the gate.
He opens the gate, returns the key, and leaves for work.
I step into my icy shower.

A LUCKY BREATH

At 7:00 AM, a man I have hired comes for me in a blue pick-up truck.
We load it with my foam mattress, my pillow, my mop and broom, my two plastic chairs, my stove burners, my pots and pans, and my clothes.
I don't even leave a note.

I cannot think of one thing to say except goodbye, and I've said it enough times.
My heart is pounding as I ride in the truck down out of San Francisco de Dos Ríos, but I know that everything is ok.
Everything is ok.
Everything is ok.

※

Moving into Angelina's house was as simple as pushing my suitcase under the extra bed in her little boy's room. Neighbors came by to say hello and how glad they were to see me again and how long was I planning to stay? I smiled, hugging and kissing them happily, and said I didn't know how long. A year, maybe? Something told me it might be more, but I needed an easy answer.

Night fell. Angelina put a plate of rice, beans, and the leg of a stewed chicken on the table for me beside a glass of sugary black coffee. There weren't enough plates or chairs for family meals, and all the brothers were never home at the same time anyway. They wandered in from time to time and ate when food was available.

That was the night I first saw Enrique. He wasn't living there the first time I came to Los Ríos to learn Spanish and pottery. He was working, then, in the banana plantations in the southern Caribbean region, sending money home to María and to Inez who was pregnant with Adán.

Angelina's sons took me with them to watch the games of dice the men and boys played in the evenings on the lopsided pool table behind a little store. I hoped The Boy would come. I wanted to see him, for him to tell me to my face about The Girl, for him to see he wasn't the only thing I loved about Los Ríos and that I wasn't going away as easily as he might think.

He didn't come. Not that night.

But there, beside Mateo and the other familiar faces, stood a man I didn't recognize. Wearing a yellow shirt and standing under the bare yellow mosquito bulb engrossed in the prediction of numbers, he seemed to glow with his own light. I knew immediately I hadn't seen this man before because I would have remembered. He was beautiful: tall, muscular, the color of rich coffee, with soft black curls that hung to his long eyelashes.

A LUCKY BREATH

Our gazes crossed and Enrique looked away, pretending to ignore me, but when I caught him watching me later his smile was timid.

Los Ríos believes in luck, and Enrique was intent on deciphering its invisible fingerprints on the little dotted cubes. When it was his turn to roll, Enrique silently passed me the cup of dice and dared me with his eyes to roll them. I took the cup from him without looking away. I blew a lucky breath into it, swirled it once, threw the dice on the table, and won the game for him.

Part IX: The Beginning

It is the beginning of August, 2000.
I move into a bright little apartment on a side street between Guadalupe and Coronado.
There are four apartments behind the tall gate, and mine is one of the two on the second level.
I feel safe up here.
Even with all the wide glass windows, I feel safe.
I live at the end of the street.
Beside the house is a rushing stream that gurgles all day and all night.
It's like music.
It is music.
A little yard lies between the apartments, with grass and pink flowers.
I have a big kitchen sink and a small counter for my stove top.
The shower has hot water.
In the bedroom, there is a dresser for my clothes and a closet with a folding door.
The windows have dark blue curtains and the walls are green.

A LUCKY BREATH

At the top of the street is a little grocery store which sells everything I need.
Across the street from the store is a bus stop.

It is a perfect place to rest my exhausted spirit.
A perfect place to hide.
It is a perfect place to talk to myself, cry, laugh, sleep, write stories, and wait.
It's a perfect place to think.
It's a perfect place to listen to the rain.
It's a perfect place for cats.
It's a perfect place to begin.

And that is what I do now.
I get some cats.
I begin.

The beginning is very quiet.
Things are a bit formless and void.
There is nothing and it seems like there never will be anything, but that is not true.
There will be everything.

I went back to college to finish my theatre degree when Study Abroad Term ended, but the dark and light of the stage were no longer the only magic that pulled me. I heard the roosters crowing, the rustle of leaves, felt the smooth warm stone in my hand, the rivulets of sweat behind my knees, the cool curve inside the mouth of the new clay vessels. Letters came to me from the potter who asked me questions I didn't know the answers to, who promised my life was in Los Ríos. I didn't know if he was wrong or right. I only knew that the last day of my life on which I had been happy, I was in Los Ríos with the potter, the clay, the hot sun, and sweet coffee brewed over a fire.

Two years later, when I graduated, I took a two-week trip back to Costa Rica. I expected to be disappointed, to realize the experience I so idealized for the past two years was not a picture of reality.

That is not what happened. The country, the air between the mountains, the lilting language, the dozens of anxious embraces, pulled me back in as if I had never been gone. The Boy was waiting for me. The trees and the hills and the sugar-flavored sunshine were waiting for me. I told The Boy I loved him but that when I left, I would marry my boyfriend.

That didn't happen, either. I arrived home destroyed. I broke up with the boyfriend I was supposed to marry, renounced an internship that would begin my career, moved back into the farmhouse with my parents, and took a job renting Halloween costumes, folding chairs, and chafing dishes. I didn't care what I had to do. Anything to get me back to Los Ríos. I wrote The Boy that I was coming back. He said he didn't know what to do without me.

For two more years, I paid college debts and put money away. Then I bought a suitcase, a ticket, Teva sandals, and extra toothpaste.

A LUCKY BREATH

The Boy who swore he would wait for me forever, didn't quite make it. A week before I boarded the plane with an inkling I might never come back, he told me on the phone about The Girl who had become his novia. A stabbing pain filled my chest, and then nausea. I held the receiver to my head and listened to the small voice stammer nervously through the static. I said it was okay. We could just be friends.

That disappointing news didn't stop me. He was one of the things I loved about Los Ríos, but not the only one. I had the ticket in my hand, I'd already said 100 good-byes, and there was no turning back. In May 1995, I got on the plane to Costa Rica, ready to find out what happens next.

Afterword I

There is much forgiveness to be done.
Some of it, I must do.
Some of it, I must ask for.

Enrique is easy to forgive.
He is the human his world shaped him to be.
As am I.
The rules he broke are my rules; they never belonged to him.

David is easy to forgive.
Our errors are so many and so entwined it is impossible to determine which belong to whom.

I ask Inez to forgive me.
The request takes years to form and is difficult.
Her pardon is immediate.

Forgiving myself is hard work.
I must start over day after day, year after year.
I write story after story, searching for a place to begin.

Afterword II

It is a hot sunny December day.
Wind rattles the palm leaves outside my windows and makes striped shade dance back and forth across the floor.
I pull a dress over my head and brush back my hair flecked with the tiniest bits of gray.
The woman in the mirror smiles at me.
It's time to go.

Today is Carina's oldest daughter's sixth birthday.
She requested a princess piñata, and fortunately, I found one.
I set a wrapped gift and the piñata stuffed with candy in the car beside me and drive from my home in Playa Celeste to Los Rios.
The birthday party will be at Inez's house where Inez, Carina, and her two little girls live.

Miguel will bring his little boy, Adán will come when work is finished, neighbor children and their parents will fill the yard, and Enrique will hang the piñata from the branch of a tree.

The road from Santa Cruz is still a corridor lined by live jocote fences.

Here is Santa Cecilia.

Each time I pass, I remember my melting shoes.

Coming into Los Rios, the pottery workshop where Miguel works with Enrique stands in the same shade.

I drive past the plaza that is irrigated, now, and green all year.

Past the Angelina's house.

Past the home where The Boy lived with his parents.

Past the turn to Mateo and Norma's house.

It all looks different than it used to, but only a little.

The trees are bigger which makes the houses seem smaller.

The children who used to play in the plaza are sitting in the shade watching their children play in the plaza.

María and Martín rest side by side in the cemetery.

I pull up in front of Inez's house.

She is sitting on a rocking chair on the porch.

Carina's girls are playing in the yard.

When they see me, they drop their toys and leap to their feet. As I step from the car, they run to me shrieking, "Abuela Diana! Abuela Diana!" and throw themselves into my arms.

ABOUT THE AUTHOR

Diana R. Zimmerman is the author of *When the Roll is Called a Pyonder, Marry a Mennonite Boy and Make Pie,* and several collections of poetry. She lives and writes in Costa Rica.